What people are saying about

Trophy Child

"Ted Cunningham brings a fresh and encouraging perspective to biblical parenting. His new book, *Trophy Child*, will give you helpful insight in preparing and equipping your children to serve God with all their hearts."

Craig Groeschel, senior pastor of
LifeChurch.tv and author of *Soul Detox:
Clean Living in a Contaminated World*

"Let's face it—parenting ain't for wimps. We need to let our kids do their own homework, learn how to lose a few games, and deal with the consequences of their decisions. This book will give you a backbone without turning you into a tiger mom."

Dr. Kevin Leman, *New York Times* best-
selling author of *Have a New Kid by Friday*

"*Trophy Child* will provide a great compass for any parent who wants to keep their children moving toward a dynamic and everyday faith."

Reggie Joiner, founder and CEO of
Orange and author of *Think Orange*

"Today's parents need massive amounts of encouragement to stay the course. My pastor and friend, Ted Cunningham, understands the t̶r̶a̶p̶ o̶f̶ p̶e̶r̶f̶o̶r̶m̶a̶n̶c̶e̶ a̶n̶d̶ p̶e̶r̶f̶e̶c̶t̶i̶o̶n that so easily ensnare parents'

motives. You will enjoy this read. Ted is a ton of fun with a solid biblical foundation."

Dr. Gary Smalley, speaker and best-selling
author of *The DNA of Relationships*

"Having kids who look out for the needs of others and who truly love and serve the Lord—that's what every Christian parent longs for! Without relying on formulas or easy answers, Ted Cunningham helps moms and dads understand what it means to instill *character* in their kids. This is a great book!"

Jim Daly, president of Focus on the Family

"*Trophy Child* is a timely resource for parents raising kids in this generation. Ted Cunningham is my pastor. He's also in the top few most gifted communicators in the speaking and writing world. Ted shares his heart and experience in a delightful, encouraging, and easy-to-read fashion. His ability to share God's truth with grace and humor is something I love about Ted."

Dr. Joe White, president of Kanakuk Kamps

"Ted Cunningham is a gifted communicator who is renewing the way this generation thinks about marriage and parenting. The thinking behind *Trophy Child* won't just make you a better mom or dad; it will make you a better follower of Jesus."

Margaret Feinberg, author of *Wonderstruck* and
Scouting the Divine, www.margaretfeinberg.com

"As a father of two sons, I am constantly looking for sources of practical wisdom and biblical truth as my wife and I raise our boys to become men of God. As I read these pages, I knew I had found a unique and helpful resource. Ted has masterfully crafted page after page of information, inspiration, correction, and application that parents can immediately put to use in their homes. Seldom does a book inspire me to talk out loud while reading it, but I caught myself over and over agreeing with Ted's observations and applications on trophy parenting and the need to prepare our children for kingdom ministry in the real world. Get this book for yourself and all your friends with kids."

Clayton King, founder and president of
Crossroads Ministries, teaching pastor
at NewSpring Church, and campus
pastor at Liberty University

"Through his conversational style with great personal illustrations, Ted Cunningham brings outstanding wisdom and insight for parents. This book is inspiring and will help you understand your parenting motives. Ted Cunningham is not only one of America's finest pastors, he has great insight into keeping families healthy."

Jim Burns, PhD, president of HomeWord and
author of *Confident Parenting* and *The Purity Code*

"Ted's words speak truth to the parents of this millennial generation. It's time to take the kids off the shelf and prepare them for something bigger than themselves (and us)."

Tim Popadic, MFT, national
director of Date Night Works

TROPHY CHILD

TROPHY CHILD

Saving Parents FROM Performance

· · · · · ·

Preparing Children FOR Something Greater THAN Themselves

TED CUNNINGHAM

David C Cook®

transforming lives together

TROPHY CHILD
Published by David C Cook
4050 Lee Vance View
Colorado Springs, CO 80918 U.S.A.

David C Cook Distribution Canada
55 Woodslee Avenue, Paris, Ontario, Canada N3L 3E5

David C Cook U.K., Kingsway Communications
Eastbourne, East Sussex BN23 6NT, England

The graphic circle C logo is a registered trademark of David C Cook.

Personal stories throughout used with permission. Some
names have been changed to protect privacy.

The website addresses recommended throughout this book are offered as a
resource to you. These websites are not intended in any way to be or imply an
endorsement on the part of David C Cook, nor do we vouch for their content.

Unless otherwise noted, Scripture quotations are taken from the Holy Bible,
New International Version®, NIV®. Copyright © 1973, 1984 by Biblica, Inc.™
Used by permission of Zondervan. All rights reserved worldwide. www.
zondervan.com. Scripture quotations marked NIV 2011 are taken from the Holy
Bible, New International Version®, NIV®. Copyright © 1973, 2011 by Biblica,
Inc.™ Used by permission of Zondervan. All rights reserved worldwide. www.
zondervan.com; NLT are taken from the *Holy Bible*, New Living Translation,
copyright © 1996, 2007 by Tyndale House Foundation. Used by permission
of Tyndale House Publishers, Inc., Carol Stream, Illinois 60188. All rights
reserved; NASB are taken from the New American Standard Bible®, Copyright
© 1960, 1995 by The Lockman Foundation. Used by permission. (www.
Lockman.org.); MSG are taken from THE MESSAGE. Copyright © by Eugene
H. Peterson 1993, 2002. Used by permission of NavPress Publishing Group.

LCCN 2012941797
ISBN 978-0-7814-0763-2
eISBN 978-1-4347-0516-7

The Team: Alex Field, Amy Konyndyk, Renada Arens, Caitlyn Carlson, Karen Athen
Cover Design: Nick Lee

Printed in the United States of America
First Edition 2012

062912

To my parents,
Ron and Bonnie Cunningham.
Thank you for leading, preparing, and launching me.
I love you!

Acknowledgments

Thank you to my friends at David C Cook. Alex Field is a true friend and fantastic encourager. Thank you to Don Pape, Terry Behimer, Ingrid Beck, Annette Brickbealer, Ginia Hairston, Caitlyn Carlson, Renada Arens, and the rest of the editorial, sales, and marketing teams for their passion and expertise. Many thanks to Lisa Beech for faithfully scheduling radio and television interviews for this book.

God has blessed me with many tremendous friends and mentors in ministry. Gary and Norma Smalley, Joe and Debbie Jo White, Jim and Judy Sedlacek, and Bill and Carolyn Rogers are key leaders in my life. Margaret Feinberg, Dan Seaborn, Josh and Christi Straub, Leonard Davidson, Michael Stewart, Johnnie Moore, Michael and Ali Hall, Steve and Barbara Uhlmann, Austin and Jennifer Deloach, Matt and Jennifer Taylor, Rob and Susan Robbins, and Roger and Kari Gibson are all gracious partners in ministry.

Woodland Hills Family Church supports my passion in fighting for marriage and family. Thank you to the elders, staff, and congregation for your hard work for marriages and families in Branson and around the world.

Finally, a big thank-you to my family. Amy, Corynn, and Carson allow their lives to be on display. I do not take that for granted. This is our ministry. Amy and I thank our own parents for the many illustrations we received from them.

Contents

Chapter 1
Trophies

Parenting is not a sport, and our children are not trophies. No performing, perfecting, comparing, or competing necessary.

My children are a wonderful blessing from the Lord and a welcomed addition to our family. They will not be with me forever, so I prepare them accordingly. It is not my goal to hold on to them for life, take credit for what God is doing through them, or show them off to family and friends.

God placed a mantle of leadership on my shoulders in 2003 with the birth of my first child, and since then I've found that parenting is a hard job. It comes with pressure, responsibility, heartache, joy, frustration, and guilt. To think that God trusts me to impress His Word on my children's hearts is scary and humbling.

Our job as parents is to raise children who love Jesus and leave home as responsible adults. We prepare them for a lifetime of following Christ, working hard, being married, and raising a family.

When kids spend their childhood years fulfilling Mom and Dad's desires and dreams, they lose out on discovering who God created them to be and what He has prepared for them to do. When parents push their personal agendas, the kids miss out on identifying their God-given personality, passions, and spiritual gifts.

Through our ministry to families at Woodland Hills Family Church in Branson, Missouri, we observe that most parents over-indulge their children, center the home around them, and in some ways turn their own children into idols. As parents, we often use anything and everything to place them on the pedestal—including their accomplishments, looks, personalities, and attributes—in order to impress others.

God blessed my wife, Amy, and me with two children, Corynn and Carson. Turning them into trophies is easy and requires little effort—trophy parenting is a piece of cake. Parenting with the right motives is difficult. We sometimes catch ourselves treating our children as extensions of ourselves.

No one else on earth is exactly like Corynn—she is unique. She has some of my personality and tendencies but is different in so many ways. She enjoys holding my hand while walking down the path to our favorite fishing hole. We snuggle on the couch at night. She is constantly painting pictures, making duct-tape phone cases, and crafting friendship bracelets for me. Corynn is my princess, but I am her father, not her BFF.

Even though he looks like me, Carson is not an extension of me. He has my sense of humor and laughs at my jokes. He splits apple fritters with me at Starbucks and practices his karate on me every day. I've got the marks to prove it. We use our backyard trampoline with safety net as a cage-fighting arena. His greatest thrill in life is flying through the air with the greatest ease to deliver a jab to my lower back. Taking down Dad is his primary goal in life. Carson is my mighty warrior, but I am his dad, not his lifelong sparring partner.

Corynn and Carson will be with me for a short time, and even though the days go slow, the years go fast. Like passing through Wahoo, Nebraska, which only takes the blink of an eye, my children will grow up and leave. During that blink, my wife and I are the primary authors of our children's hearts. My concern during this short time is impressing a love for the Lord on their hearts, rather than impressing others with my parenting. Leading my children in daily devotions, loving their mom, and encouraging their personal commitment to Jesus Christ far outweighs their ACT scores, choice of college, or performance in sports or extracurricular activities.

In the past, I was a trophy collector, both in sports and parenting. That nonsense stops here and now.

My Not-So-Stellar Athletic Career

I was one of the greatest athletes of the twentieth century. Ha! Actually, my role *was* vitally important in getting the Oswego Panthers cross-country team to the Illinois State Finals. Double Ha!

I was the alternate. Let me explain.

At every meet, each school ran seven guys. For the Panthers, I was number eight. That meant I was ready at a moment's notice if one of the top seven suffered illness or injury. At most races and invitational events I sat on the sidelines, cheering on my teammates and praying that they would stay healthy. There's no greater feeling than bundling up in forty-degree weather, enjoying a cup of hot chocolate, and watching hundreds of the state's top runners compete. It was a good place for me to be.

During the regular season, each hosting school held a second race after the main invitational each Saturday. They called it the Open. I called it the scrub race, even though I was a top runner in that competition. The Open gave trophies to the top five runners— nothing fancy, just a plastic runner standing (or running, rather) on a marble base. No columns or placards. It felt so obligatory; they handed you your trophy the moment you crossed the finish line. There was no awards ceremony.

The Open was an unnecessary race. It usually ran after the main event to give the event coordinators time to clean up the race site. It also gave the primary runners time for their cooldown. There's nothing more embarrassing than being passed during the race by a runner from the previous race—as he's doing his cooldown. *Ouch!*

Try harder. Lift more. Focus. "Dedication, Pride, and Tradition" was our motto. Despite lots of effort on my part, I was and continue to be a not-so-stellar athlete. But I prayed for my team during every race and cheered them home during the Illinois State Finals.

There was another sport I participated in toward the end of high school. I had a short stint in powerlifting. Most people seem shocked when I tell them that because I am not Red Lobster's fresh catch of the day and could stand to lose a couple pounds, but it's true.

My high school shop teacher, Mr. Groth, was a passionate guy who bench-pressed over five hundred pounds. He was a great mentor and friend who invested in me during my four years in high school.

I lifted competitively at eighteen, shortly after my high school graduation. My short career ended one year later, right before I turned twenty. I was a horrible powerlifter, but I received trophies for participation anyway.

Catching the theme yet?

Competitive powerlifting has two main categories: age and weight. Within each of those categories are too many divisions to count. I lifted in the teen division at 165 pounds.

My first meet was in Plano, Illinois, at a car dealership. I kid you not—they cleared the cars from the showroom floor and made room for seats, a platform, and an impressive trophy display. When I say trophy display, I mean it was massive! The smallest trophy was over two feet tall, a long way from the four-inch cross-country trophies I collected. The first-place trophies stood over three-and-half-feet tall.

There was only one other kid in my division, which guaranteed me a two-and-a-half-foot trophy. Hot diggity! Mr. Groth had brought a team of six guys, and they were each genuinely happy for me, knowing that trophy was mine. We had no idea that the three-and-a-half-foot trophy had Ted Cunningham's name on it. All the credit goes to Mr. Groth.

He pulled me aside at the registration table and said, "Ted, let's start with a weight you can nail no sweat. You get three lifts, and it is critical that you get at least one weight posted. If no weight is posted, that means no trophy." Understood.

He was the coach, so I started at 225 pounds on the bench.

My competitor was a confident young stud with a bad coach. His starting weight was 300, and he missed it all three times. I hit

225, then 250, then 275. When they called me up for the trophy, Mr. Groth and all my buddies went nuts.

As we left the event, I turned around and looked at the remains of the trophy display—and there sat the two-and-a-half-foot trophy for second place in my division, which went unclaimed. What happened? Did I really win? Is it a stretch to say I was good at powerlifting and deserved a three-and-a-half-foot trophy? My coach deserved it more than I did.

Nonetheless, I was hooked. I went on to compete professionally at twelve more events. That's an exaggerated statement, but it builds anticipation for where I am landing this story.

For me, powerlifting became less about competing and more about collecting trophies. I found myself registering for the novice, open, and teen divisions at each event. Three divisions meant three trophies. My shelf was full. Six years after I retired from powerlifting, I got a dreaded phone call from my mom.

"Dad is turning your bedroom into a reading room for me and wants to get rid of all these trophies," she said. And for the life of me, I could not see her sending me those megahuge, unearned trophies.

"Just throw them away," I said.

"I hate to do that with all the time and money you spent on getting these," she responded. Way to rub it in, Mom!

The next year at Christmas, my family presented me with a display shelf that my brother had built. On this custom shelf sat the bulky plastic men that had once crowned those massive trophies. I chuckled. My parents had had my brother unscrew the guys from the tops of each trophy and fasten them to this beautiful fireplace-looking mantle.

After my family left our house, my wife looked at me and asked, "You are not seriously considering hanging that mantle in this house, are you?"

"Thanks for your support, honey," I quickly responded.

There you have it. Now you know. I was not one of the greatest athletes of the twentieth century. I am not an athlete by any stretch of the imagination. I am a recovering trophy collector. You are reading a book written by a nonathlete. Now the question is—did my kids get my genes?

On Display

We award trophies to teams and individuals who excel in a sport or activity. We've seen them hoisted by athletes, displayed on mantles, and lined up in cases outside of school gymnasiums. There are trophies for bowling, running, racing, beauty, and dancing. You can get one for participating, placing, completing, or winning. Some movie stars dedicate an entire room in their homes to one trophy. Takes ego and cash to do something like that. Like Billy Crystal said at the 2012 Oscar awards, "Nothing can take the sting out of the world's economic problems like watching millionaires present each other with golden statues."

We earn awards, collect them, display them, brag about them, reminisce over them, and toss them out.

There is a new kind of trophy being sought by parents. It's the prize that is our children. Bumper stickers, Facebook and Twitter posts, unlimited opportunities, no-loser competitions, and excessive praise elevate our children to a whole new level of recognition. They do not stand on shelves, but everything they do is on display.

I'll never forget when the doctor first displayed our firstborn. She was four weeks old, and during her first doctor's visit, they measured her weight, height, and head circumference and compared her to every other infant in the nation. Amy and I peered over the doctor's shoulder at the computer monitor as he explained that the circumference of Corynn's head was in the ninety-eighth percentile. *Yeah!*

I remember asking Amy, "Why do we care how Corynn's head circumference lines up with the rest of the world? And oh yeah, what do we need to do to beat out that other two percent?"

Corynn's weight was another story. She was underweight, and that caused us a great deal of concern. When the doctor recommended we supplement Corynn's nursing with formula, I thought it was a good idea. But I soon received unsolicited opinions from parents on the pros and cons of formula—and it didn't stop there. We compared ourselves to other parents over the use of pacifiers, diapers, potty-training techniques, and training wheels.

Parents of previous generations had different stresses. Many parents felt blessed if their children went to bed at night with a full stomach. These parents survived wars and depressions and prioritized the important stuff, while we take for granted those things for which our grandparents praised their Father in heaven. My grandparents were patriotic, sacrificial, dutiful, loyal, God-honoring, and faithful blue-collar workers. Their parenting plan was simple, and their goal was to pass their values on to their family.

The shift started around 1980 and continues today with the phenomenon of the kid-centered home. Parents began shifting their style to be more encouraging, nurturing, and praising, bombarding kids with excessive "atta-boys," gold stars for every paper, no-loser competitions, no-failure-allowed assignments, big moments on the stage or field, and plenty of opportunity and privilege. Most of our strategies are the same as those of our parents and grandparents, but our values are not.

The shift toward the kid-centered home has many roots, but divorce is one of the leading causes of the kid-centered home and the raising of trophy children. Parents elevate their children to adult or companion status, and they require their kids to bear a burdensome emotional load.

Your own childhood often determines much of your parenting style. If parents grew up in an abusive or neglectful home, they compensate for their own childhood experiences by overencouraging their children.

Parents misinterpret love. They believe they are doing their children a service by elevating them and overencouraging them. They believe this is the best way to communicate love, not realizing the damage caused by revolving the world around their children.

The "miracle child" syndrome is another example of the kid-centered home. Parents who struggled with infertility prior to having a child often refer to their child as a miracle. They hold on to them with fierce diligence rather than letting go and trusting God with their children.

The motives of the modern parent weren't seen in other generations. Again, we share strategies similar to those used by past generations, but we deploy those strategies with radically different motives. There are five primary motives of parents who display their children.

Motive #1: We Obsess over Achievement and Competition

This first motive launches our children into organized activities before they have developed necessary social skills and the ability to handle change. We place our children in competitive sports at early ages and forget how important it is for them to enjoy free playtime in those early childhood development years:

> As kids participate in organized, competitive programs at increasingly early ages ... "they don't learn how to get along. The coach says, 'You come here; you go there.' Everything is directed from the adults' point of view. In the informal play settings of past generations, kids had to learn how to negotiate with other kids...." The activities of today's children are so carefully directed ... that they have little opportunity to develop life-negotiation skills.[1]

Remember when kids went up the street to play at a neighbor's house? How about setting up a piece of plywood in the ditch and jumping bikes for hours? Those were the days. Summer was incomplete without one friend wearing something in a cast.

Now, our obsession includes praising every attempt, activity, and achievement regardless of outcome, so much so that attempt and achievement actually become synonymous. We give trophies and ribbons for trying, not necessarily placing or even finishing. We reward success and minimize failure. We do not accept weakness or rejection. If someone rejects our child or places him or her on the wrong team, we write it off as another's problem.

Excessive praise can lead to apathy and an inflated view of self, especially when we exaggerate the skills, talents, and giftedness of our own children. Average isn't good enough. They begin to feel as if they must strive to be gifted (*at everything*).

Branson, Missouri, is known for great live entertainment. Locals call it Hillbilly Vegas. One of my family's favorite dinner shows is the Dixie Stampede. You eat a chicken dinner with your fingers while watching a fantastic rodeo-style show. Doesn't get any better than that in Branson, Missouri!

The show is set during the Civil War, and the organizers divide the audience into two teams—North and South. The emcee rides on a beautiful mare and keeps the audience fully engaged by pitting one side against the other. After the equestrian riders compete, the emcee invites the audience to participate. He chooses members from the audience to compete in toilet-seat-lid horseshoes and couples' tandem horse races on sticks. At the end of each adult competition, the winners receive medals.

The final competition is a chicken-chase race for children. It is hilarious entertainment. Four children are selected—two from the North and two from the South—and they are each given a chicken to chase across the finish line. Depending on the temperament of the chickens (and the children), the emcee offers his assistance.

At the end of the race, a winner is declared. A mixture of boos and cheers flow from the crowd. Then the emcee pulls two shiny medals out of his pocket and places them on the winning team. But wait, there's more. He pulls out two identical medals and says, "We believe all children are winners." The crowd erupts with applause, and all four winners leave the arena. I cringe, and my lower lip starts quivering.

At that point my wife looks at me because she knows what I'm thinking.

I am stewing with thoughts like, *They are not all winners. Two won, and two lost. You're not doing these kids any favors by declaring them all winners. Let's prepare them for life with a healthy dose of reality. Those kids need to leave here knowing that they are not good chicken chasers. Tell them the truth, for heaven's sake!*

Amy responds with, "Ted, it's just a chicken-chase race."

She is right; I need to learn how to relax. They give out these medals because all four kids had the courage to stand up and chase chickens in front of a large audience of strangers.

However, I never want to rob my children of loss and disappointment in the early stages of life. Loss, failure, pain, and trials build character in our kids. Each one of us has a tale of major heartache that is part of our story. Why in the world would I want to deprive my children of healthy character development, even if it's just them learning how to deal with losing a chicken-chase race?

Motive #2: We Create Environments Where Our Kids Can Succeed Rather Than Preparing Them for Environments They Cannot Control

Stephanie Watson is a mom and the children's ministry director at Woodland Hills Family Church. When she heard I was writing a book called *Trophy Child*, she reacted cautiously.

"What's your thesis?" she asked.

I said, "Children have become an extension of their parents. Mom and Dad exhaust themselves with the performance of their children. They offer constant praise in an attempt to build self-esteem. We have placed our children in the driver's seat."

Stephanie gave me the "I hope you're wrong" look. She was vulnerable enough with me to share her best trophy child parenting moment.

Ever since her son Sam was three, he played every sport offered. Each season ended with an awards ceremony, and each child received a trophy or medal. Lucy, Sam's younger sister, watched these presentations with great anticipation for years.

Lucy is quite the little athlete, but unfortunately she chose one sport that refrained from participatory awards: gymnastics. While Sam's dresser filled up with his trophy collection, Lucy's remained empty.

Each summer, the Watson family enjoyed Toad Suck Daze, an annual event in their hometown of Conway, Arkansas, and every Toad Suck festival featured toad races. When Lucy was five years old, she entered her prize toad in the races and made it to the finals. The grand-prize trophy for the final toad race was so huge that a five-year-old would need parental help to hold it up. Wouldn't you know it, Lucy's toad came in second place. No trophy.

Lucy was heartbroken. Yet another trophy had slipped through her fingers. What should a loving, nurturing mom do? Sit there and do nothing? No, not Stephanie Watson—she hatched a plan. As she put it, "My baby's self-esteem was not going to be affected by a toad race."

At the next gymnastics class, Stephanie talked to the coach about performing a private awards ceremony for Lucy. The coach agreed so long as Stephanie provided the trophy or certificate.

After Lucy's last class before the Watsons moved to Branson, the gymnastics coach presented Lucy with her first award, a seven-dollar trophy that Stephanie had purchased.

Creating environments for our kids to succeed makes sense to most parents. It feels loving. We pick schools, churches, leagues, neighborhoods, and family friends based on this principle.

Is this the best approach?

I posted this question on Facebook several months back: "Are you creating environments for your children to succeed or teaching them how to get along in environments they cannot control?"

One parent responded with, "Hopefully both."

But where's that line?

Motive #3: We Accelerate Childhood Milestones and Delay Adulthood Milestones

There is an interesting rhythm in the home today. We attempt to speed up our children's early development, but then later in life we put on the brakes when they are ready to be launched into adulthood.

I remember watching the *My Baby Can Read* commercials before we had children and thinking to myself, *Babies say goo-goo, ga-ga … why do they need to read? Is a well-read baby about the baby or about Mommy and Daddy?* I prefer the Chuck E. Cheese commercial and motto: "Where a kid can be a kid."

We want our children to live up to their potential even when we do not know what their potential is at age one. While accelerating their development and growth, we tend to exaggerate their stage in life.

My wife is the family ministries' director at our church, so she is responsible for all children's ministries, birth through high school. We organize our children's programs by grade in school, not birth date, and we regularly hear from parents who believe their child is far more advanced than the other children in the class.

A very kind and loving mom pulled my wife aside one Sunday and said, "My daughter is in second grade but relationally, intellectually, and emotionally functions more like a fourth grader."

Seriously?

We have no formal policy, but my wife's unspoken policy is "no special treatment, regardless of the circumstances." Instead of letting the child switch classes, Amy encourages the parents to let the child lead in the classroom. So if you are one of those parents, beware. It's not as though your son or daughter can catch a lower IQ like catching a cold.

Why the rush in the early years of development? Why are parents frantic over their kids advancing intellectually, emotionally, and relationally? We prepare them for the American dream while they are still in diapers and continue it through the school years.

Parents "launch their son or daughter on a trajectory of success by following the popular performance scenario of getting good grades in school, getting into a good college, getting a good job, and getting a good living, thereby fulfilling the American dream of materially doing well," said Carl E. Pickhardt in his article on vanity parenting for *Psychology Today*.[2]

We accelerate the early milestones until the tween years. But from ages ten to thirteen, children begin individualizing, and parents freak out. Younger children are more compliant and always seek approval from Mom and Dad. When they display adult-like qualities, we begin slowing them down. We use phrases like, "She's twelve going on twenty." *Is that such a bad thing?* We pushed them for years to grow up in every way. Now we should allow them to develop their own opinions, tastes, personality, likes, and dislikes. Add responsibility to those things. Guide them through relationships. Get them employed. Refuse to prolong their childhood or adolescence.

When they show signs of launching, let them soar. I once heard the story of a child learning to ride a horse. To get the horse moving, she would squeeze her legs and spur the horse as instructed. Then in fear, she would pull back on the reigns. The horse grew frustrated and confused. Often our kids feel the same way. We push them to get moving, then pull back on the reigns when they show signs of galloping.

Motive #4: We Take Too Much Credit and Too Much Blame for the Way Our Kids Turn Out

The faulty input/output parenting theory teaches that what we put into our child is what we get out. Christian parents know the verse "Train a child in the way he should go, and when he is old he will not turn from it" (Prov. 22:6). That verse causes many sleepless nights for parents. Parents of adult children cringe each time it is quoted in church as they reflect on the life of a child who chose a lifestyle far away from Jesus.

We falsely interpret that proverb as a guarantee or promise, rather than as a general understanding. Another example of that kind of interpretation method is Proverbs 10:4: "Lazy hands make a man poor, but diligent hands bring wealth." I know plenty of hard workers who struggle financially. Diligence instead of laziness simply gives you a better shot at success. The same is true of parenting.

Since I'm a pastor, an extra verse hits me from the qualifications list for church leadership in 1 Timothy 3: "He must manage his own family well and see that his children obey him with proper respect. (If anyone does not know how to manage his own family, how can he take care of God's church?)" (vv. 4–5). Pastors lose sleep over those verses for two reasons. One, they truly love their family and fear that the church will prevent or destroy that close-knit bond. Second, they fear loss of job and income.

Parents are the primary influence in raising their children. However, there are many other influences to consider: teachers, coaches, pastors, friends, movies, music, personality, learning styles, IQ, social exposure, world events, and of course, a child's own free will. In other words, we parents are not the only "inputs" our children receive.

Parents are sinful. I have flaws. You have flaws. We make mistakes and wrong choices. We raise our voices when tired, angry, or distracted. We jump to conclusions. We fly off the handle. We discipline hastily when exhausted.

One of the hidden blessings of taking your child down off the shelf and no longer treating him or her as a trophy is giving yourself room to breathe. Try it right now. Take a deep breath. Hold it. Count to three. Now let it out. You need those breaths several times a day.

Just like you, your children are not perfect. No matter how hard you try, they never will be. Breathe, my friend.

Motive #5: We Connect with Our Children More Frequently and for Longer Periods of Time

At some point in our parenting journey, it comes time to cut the strings.

My family loves the ocean. When we go to the beach, we spend hours running into the waves, burying the kids in the sand, and looking for seashells. When Amy and I tire out we sit back on a couple of beach chairs under an umbrella and watch the kids for a few more hours.

Recently we traveled to Pensacola Beach, Florida. As the sun set, Amy and I watched the kids from a safe distance.

High tide was rolling in when Amy asked me, "Do you think they are getting a little too far out?" My wife watches too many shark-attack shows on the Discovery Channel. She dreads the creatures of the sea and rarely goes out past her ankles.

"They're fine," I replied.

"How fast could you get to them if they were swept out?" she asked.

"Less than five seconds," I assured her.

"That would be too late," she said.

"Cut the strings, Amy. Our kids are strong swimmers. Let them venture out a bit," I encouraged her. She shook her head, but I saw her landing the parental helicopter.

"You're right. I know it is more about me and my fears than it is about them," she admitted.

What a great place to ask some deep questions. Is your hovering over your kids about them or about you? If you refuse to "cut the strings," who is it really about?

We wrapped up our conversation with a relaxed sigh and an "aww" when we saw them in the surf, holding hands and battling waves. It was a Kodak moment.

Our "we have made the right decision" sigh came to a screeching halt when Carson ran up the beach, screaming.

"Mom, I got scratched by a shell," he yelled while holding his back. I knew immediately that it was no shell. It was his first jellyfish sting. I had seen the creatures earlier scattered like land mines all over the beach.

"Where did you get scratched, Carson? Show me," I requested. He turned around and showed me a red mark in the middle of his back.

"You are not going to like what I have to say, Carson. I think you have a jellyfish sting. Daddy needs to pee on your back," I told him.

He thought I was kidding.

After I explained the age-old remedy for a jellyfish sting, he said, "I'll just pee in a cup and pour it on myself." I like that. He is thinking for himself.

This final motive confuses most parents because close-knit families who spend a lot of time together are loving. It's not about a child who gets up in the middle of the night to come join you in bed or one who has separation anxiety when dropped off at Grandma's house. This fifth motive can negatively affect the parents' marriage and, if excessive, denies children the necessary skills for launching into adulthood.

Loving parents who prioritize their children over their marriage give all of their time, energy, money, and words to the kids and give each other the leftovers. This is an unloving act for everyone involved.

The greatest gift you can give your children is a mom and dad who love and enjoy each other. It provides kids with a support structure as they receive nurturing, care, and security from parents in a thriving marriage. The bond between husband and wife is to be stronger than the bond between a parent and a child (Gen. 2:24).

I counsel countless couples who struggle with this priority.

Jenny and her husband were at the end of their marriage. Their daughter had a few years left in high school before she would head off to college. In Jenny's mind, her husband and their marriage were not priorities. Her daughter would soon be gone. She flat out told me, "We'll work on this marriage when she leaves. He's had his chance; now he can wait."

My answer to that statement was, "That is a misplaced priority. Tension in the home helps no one. Work on the marriage, model the gospel of Jesus, and send your daughter off with the peace of knowing her mom and dad love each other and know how to work through conflict and rough spots."

It's easy when the marriage goes south, to overattach to the kids. If you're not careful, overattachment to kids can lead to a passionless marriage. Even single parents need this priority. Be open to marriage or remarriage and other relationships rather than giving all of who you are to your child. It will help you and your child for the rest of your lives.

My Confession

This is a book about parenting motives more than parenting strategies. This book is more about the parent than the child.

Most parenting books teach skills. My goal is to get you to rethink what you believe about yourself and your child. I hope you acquire some new parenting strategies, but more than that I pray you develop deep convictions and a strong theology about parents and children.

The priority of this book is not to provide discipline strategies that simply produce a more obedient child. I don't want to help you choose a style of parenting that fits your child's particular personality. I will be of no help in assessing your child's academic path or career goals.

I have not raised teenagers, and I do not have adult children. I am a husband of fifteen years, a father of a six-year-old and an eight-year-old, and a pastor of a growing church in Branson, Missouri. This book will at times feel like a diary of my trophy child parenting experiences, so you will read about every tendency, action, and outcome of narcissistic parenting of which I am already guilty.

Whenever I speak to fellow parents on the subject of raising kids who love Jesus, I always get at least one who says, "I can't wait until Ted has teenagers of his own, and then he'll see how tough it is." It is as though they want my teen to struggle and validate their pain. I get it. Parenting is a challenge. I can and do validate their pain. But nonetheless, we must speak with authority and proclaim truth into our parenting beliefs.

I am a parent and a pastor who chooses to buck the system. I refuse to go with the flow. I hope you will do the same. Together, let us take the kids down off the shelf and prepare them for something bigger than themselves (and us). Let us avoid raising children who just achieve and accomplish to no real end.

I fear I am raising trophy collectors. Last summer my son played soccer at our local YMCA. Carson tried to like soccer but did not. But he knew every competitor received a trophy at the last game. He made sure his mom and I knew when the final game of the season was on the schedule.

When we arrived at the last game, imagine our excitement when the opposing team was absent. No show means forfeit. Forfeit means automatic win. Carson lit up when he heard, "Sorry folks; no game today." We received our trophies and headed home.

The apple does not fall far from the tree.

Parent Gut Check

Since this book is more about parenting motives than parenting strategies, make Psalm 139:23–24 your prayer today:

> Search me, O God, and know my heart;
>   test me and know my anxious thoughts.
> See if there is any offensive way in me,
>   and lead me in the way everlasting.

My prayer is that you get a gut check on your parenting motives and remove your guilt-prone tendencies. Your guilt-prone parenting days are over, in Jesus's name! Let us pray together that your child will come to know Jesus and walk in His ways. Ending the trophy child syndrome is more about what you avoid than what you do.

There will be Gut Check questions at the end of each chapter of this book for you to prayerfully consider. I encourage you to stop for a moment and seek the Lord on each question. Allow the Holy Spirit to call you by name. Allow the Lord to give you some fresh vision for your son or daughter.

- How were you raised? What was your home environment like? How has that affected your view of children?
- List a few words that would describe each of your children.
- What are your primary goals in raising your children?
- What causes you guilt as a parent?
- Is there anything you are blaming yourself for?
- Which strings need to be cut?
- Which environments are you seeking to control in your child's life?

Chapter 2
Trophy Parents

My friend Ryan Pannell is a licensed marriage and family therapist who specializes in parent-teen relationships. He told me, "Trophy children are never really about the children as much as they are about the parent. I've never seen a parent with great self-worth and confidence raise a trophy kid. Raising a trophy kid has two pursuits: one, a parent finding their identity or self-worth in their children and their accomplishments, and two, a parent finding a companion in their children."[1]

Trophy parents keep high standards and expectations. We constantly raise the bar for our children and challenge them to excel. Most performance parents are well-intentioned. We want the best for our kids, but often our drive for the best exhausts both the kids and us.

We swing between two extremes. On one side we are very cut and dry, black and white. On the other side we are permissive, warm and appeasing, depending on the desired outcome. We want our kids to be "raised right," but all too often we have motives beneath the surface that we don't fully understand.

When I came to the realization that I was a trophy parent, I thought there was only one kind. But the more I work with parents, the more I realize that we come in many shapes and sizes. Maybe you are like me and exhibit one or more of the following parenting tendencies.

The Vanity Parent

Last summer I bought a canoe. It's old and has a few small leaks, but it's a great investment in our family. The kayak shop asked $195, and I talked them down to $100.

Our house is a half mile as the crow flies from Lake Taneycomo. With pruning shears, a machete, and clippers, we cut a path through the woods that leads to an Ozarkian paradise. After dragging that old canoe down our three-quarter-mile trail, all four of us piled in and set sail on our maiden voyage. We quickly learned that this was a rickety boat built for two. At first, no one moved or breathed. The slightest shift in weight meant that we might be swimming back to shore. Since Taneycomo is sixty degrees all year round, we sat so still, it felt as if we floated on driftwood amidst an ocean of sharks.

On our first trip, we fished, laughed, paddled, and explored, and ultimately, we made memories worth repeating. To this day, we hike through the woods and paddle down our private arm of the lake several nights a week.

Whenever I get super excited about something new, I share it with everyone. And usually the congregation at Woodland Hills Family Church is my primary target. One Sunday I shared the many adventures of canoeing with Swiss Family Cunningham, and my enthusiasm got the best of me.

Dr. Joe White, a member of our congregation, attended that Sunday and caught my vision for family canoeing. Joe runs Kanakuk Kamps in Branson, Missouri. Kanakuk is a summer sports camp that ministers to twenty thousand kids a year. Joe is "kidzy" and "outdoorzy" to say the least. Dr. James Dobson, founder of Focus on the Family, once said, "No one knows more about kids than Joe White." Joe has written many books on parenting and was a keynote speaker at Promise Keepers men's conferences for over a decade. Suffice it to say that he knows a thing or two about successful parenting strategies.

Sweat beads ran down my face after he called me on Monday afternoon and invited himself to join the kids and me on our canoe voyage. My first thought was, *You are not invited, Joe.* But he is a very difficult guy to turn down.

The only thing worse than Joe being the fourth member on our family's canoe trip would be Dave Ramsey spending a couple of hours with Amy and me on our budget. And why don't we invite Bobby Flay over for dinner while we're at it?

Previous trips to the canoe were laid back. Not this trip. Questions flooded my brain. *Would the kids get along? Would they be polite? Speak kindly? Take turns? Not interrupt? Respect Joe? Avoid all forms of whining? Require no corrective measures?*

Bottom line: I wanted Joe to think I am a great parent. After all that flooded my mind I thought to myself, *Jump off the back porch and sprain your ankle, Ted—then you'll have an excuse not to go.*

Joe and I travel and speak together at events around the country, and he has heard all of my stories. Like many speakers, I often share stories about rough or difficult human moments, which tend to be humorous. However, somebody seeing it in living color is entirely different. Joe knows all of my stories, but now he would experience my family firsthand.

When our kids heard Mr. Joe was coming they started gathering up their life vests, fishing poles, and walking sticks. When Joe pulled up the driveway, he experienced two excited kids and one nervous dad. My respect and honor for Joe runs deep. So mix it all together, and I was a nervous wreck!

We were not one minute into our hike when Joe said to my five-year-old, "Carson, call me Uncle Joe."

"You're not in my family," Carson responded. I froze in horror without making eye contact with Joe. While I thought of something to say or do to change the subject, Joe beat me to it.

"Carson, trust me, you want me in your family," he said. Joe is a fun and generous "uncle," if you know what I mean.

Other than that, the hike down was good with no incidents, but the first fight broke out when we saw the canoe. Corynn and Carson's excitement to show Uncle Joe the canoe turned into a fight over who would get there first. My firstborn, Corynn, went into her disciplinarian mode and corrected Carson's behavior. Carson does not warm up to Corynn's discipline. He would have none of it.

We hung out on the lake for a couple hours, and I reacted to all the kids' outbursts in that "mutter-under-your-breath, stare-down" kind of mode. You know that mode? When you get your kids' attention in a strong, subtle way so as not to draw attention to yourself? I was on edge the entire time.

When we got home, I told Amy, "That was an exhausting evening. Major stress!"

"I get it," Amy comforted me. She understood because she shares my "vanity parenting" tendencies.

The next day Joe called me to thank me for a great night. I could tell he called to comfort and affirm me more than to thank me. He knew my stress. Joe has two primary spiritual gifts: exhortation and mercy. He has the perfect gift mix for working with kids, families, and his own stressed-out pastor.

"You've got great kids, Ted," he said, and I was relieved. That's like getting a "you've got a fantastic voice" by Simon Cowell on *The X Factor*. He ended the call by saying, "The apple doesn't fall far from the tree, does it?"

I breathed a final sigh of relief.

Carl Pickhardt asked, "What is vanity parenting? When parents look to their child to bring them credit in the eyes of the world, when they push their child to reflect well on themselves, they are at risk of 'vanity parenting,' of using the child's performance to embellish their own."[2]

Vanity is a synonym for narcissism. Defined in psychological terms, narcissism is "extreme selfishness with a grandiose view of one's own talents and a craving for admiration."[3]

"To a certain extent, every child is to his or her parents a narcissistic object," said Vivian Friedman, PhD. "This means that parents feel good when their children are smart, attractive, and successful, and they feel bad when their kids are in trouble at school and other parents are complaining about them."[4]

When children become an extension of their narcissistic parents, we call them trophies. The trophy child suffers as a result of trying to meet Mom and Dad's emotional and relational needs, which comes out in our discipline strategies, the choosing of sports, and the chasing of the American dream as fuel for the parents' image. Children become high achievers or obedient but still feel as though they do not measure up.

The Perfection Parent

Corynn is my firstborn, and she places higher expectations on herself than we do. She wants perfect behavior marks and grades every day at school. Any form of correction or criticism says to her, "You are not measuring up."

We help her with math problems and spelling words each week. Getting the problems or words right is not enough. The speed of completion is equally important to her. It stresses me out. Remember when reading was the goal? Not anymore. Now we have accelerated reading.

Nighttime is tough, especially right before bed. Each night we enjoy rest time, dinner, family devotionals, and a little television. Moments before bed, I see it in Corynn's eyes—the look that says, "Am I ready for school tomorrow?" Homework is already completed, but the "did I do it right, and will I get it perfect?" sets in.

The other morning I sat at breakfast with Corynn and told her, "Sweetie, you have your daddy's personality. You have drive and passion, but a very hard time letting yourself make mistakes. I want you to know making mistakes is okay. I fear mistakes at times so much that I am sick to my stomach. I don't want that for you. Do you know what Daddy is saying?"

"I think so, Dad, but I just want Ms. Ramer to be happy with me," she replied.

"Corynn, what does the dog teach us in the Bible?" I asked.

"Don't make me say it," she said with a slight scream and smile.

"Say it, say it, say it," I humorously demanded.

She refused to say Proverbs 26:11, so I said the verse for her: "As a dog returns to its vomit, so a fool repeats his folly."

"Do we allow mistakes in this house?" I asked.

"Yes," she said.

"What don't we allow?" I prodded.

"Repeating the same mistake over and over again," she answered.

Proverbs 26:11 is part of our regular family devotions. This verse teaches that a fool makes the same mistake repeatedly, while a wise person learns from his or her mistakes. We all make mistakes. The real issue is whether we learn from them. In the Cunningham home we allow mistakes. Shoot, we even welcome them. They are great teachers.

Parents raising trophy kids experience frequent irritation and frustration when their kids mess up because expectations are too high. To resolve their frustration they speak louder and repeat themselves. The issue is not that their kids are "not getting it," but rather that the expectations are misplaced.

When parental perfection is the driver, children become responsible not for themselves but for their parents' emotional stability. For example, a child who comes home with a C on a report card experiences disappointed parents. The disappointment does not lie in the grade itself but in the parents' "we know he's a smart kid" belief. He has to be smart, because anything else implies they birthed and raised an unintelligent child.

Healthy parents know how to separate bad performance from the child's worth. They are also able to separate a child's poor performance from their own worth. They can encourage their kids to do better with an appropriate emotional investment in each child's performance.

Another effect of years in the spotlight and chasing perfection is this: trophy children can become narcissistic. They develop an overinflated sense of self-importance. Rules are for others, not them. They are the center of attention and see themselves as superior to others, which leads to entitlement. They expect to move through school, jobs, and sports without earning it, and they have difficulty looking beyond themselves to the good of others or the community.

On the other hand, not all performance-driven parents care what others think. My wife regularly confesses her trophy child pursuits, but her motives are not to impress family or friends. She is driven by the desire to see her children reach their full potential. Knowing their full potential and wanting them to achieve it, while still avoiding trophy parenting—now that is the hard part.

This quest for perfection leads to two styles of parenting: authoritarian and authoritative.

The *authoritarian style* is dominant with no room for questioning or second-guessing. In this style of parenting, children are expected to follow the strict rules established by the parents. Failure to follow such rules usually results in punishment. Authoritarian parents fail to explain the reasoning behind these rules. If asked to explain, the parent might simply reply, "Because I said so." These parents have high demands but are not responsive to their children. According to Diana Baumrind, these parents "are obedience- and status-oriented, and expect their orders to be obeyed without explanation."[5]

The *authoritative style* is firm and loving and leaves room for input from the child. This parenting style is much more democratic. Authoritative parents are responsive to their children and willing to listen to questions. When children fail to meet their expectations, authoritative parents are more nurturing and forgiving rather than punishing. Baumrind suggested that these parents "monitor and impart clear standards for their children's conduct. They are assertive, but not intrusive and restrictive. Their disciplinary methods are supportive, rather than punitive. They want their children to be assertive as well as socially responsible, and self-regulated as well as cooperative."[6]

The perfection parent is often the most guilt-prone and dominant parent. Not only are the standards too high for the child, but they are too high for the parent as well. Perfection is not possible. The constant push for performance and achievement leaves both parent and child angry, stressed, hurt, and frustrated.

The Competitive Parent

This trophy parent moves quickly from assessment to comparison. We get two outcomes when we compare ourselves (or our kids) with others: we either swell with pride and arrogance as we elevate our child above another, or we feel the emotions of inferiority and worthlessness as we place our child beneath another. Neither result is positive.

"How are the kids?"

Every parent knows this question. It seems innocent and caring, but there are only two ways to answer that question. Depending on the depth of the relationship with the asker, we can either give a laundry list of successes and achievements, or we can venture into a more vulnerable, authentic answer.

"Corynn is doing great! She just finished dance for the year with a recital last week. We have birthday parties, church activities, and play dates to keep us busy all summer. She got Mrs. Moore as a teacher for kindergarten, so we are excited about that." That would be the most elevated and positive answer.

What about a vulnerable answer?

Here's one you might not see on Facebook. "My son is struggling in school. He was cut from the baseball team and went over to track and field. He starts community college next fall. We are hoping he gets accepted. His girlfriend broke up with him last week, so he won't be going to the prom. Pray for him. He is going through a rough time."

Facebook and other types of social media are stressful outlets for the competitive parent. If you're one who struggles with envy while reading the posts of other parents on Facebook, please keep in mind that most posts are "best foot forward." Comparing our children with the status updates of others is like women comparing themselves with magazine supermodels. It's not real! On social media, people post carefully edited versions of their lives and create their own realities.

We all want our children to succeed, and that often means being the best at something. One of the struggles with organized sports is that no matter how much we push teamwork, our kids develop a "me over the good of the group" attitude.

Andy and Stephanie Watson understand this all too well. They have two thirteen-year-old boys who are passionate football players.

Sam was an Arkansas Razorbacks fan from the time he was two. The Watson family adopted Roy when he was ten, and he had no choice but to become a Razorbacks fan as well.

Sam and Roy are both skilled athletes. Sam is a quarterback, Roy is a running back, and they both play for the Branson Junior High Pirates. *Go Red and Black!*

At the start of their seventh-grade season, the coach had to make some hard decisions. With multiple kids trying out for a single position, someone always takes the top spot. Sam would not be the starting quarterback. This hit Sam hard, but it hit his mom harder. Why? It was difficult because the coach made Roy the starting running back. It is one thing to compare your child to someone across town—it is near impossible when the two competing players share a bedroom.

Andy Watson is a great dad, and I admire him greatly for the way he loves and supports his boys. With this new development in his family, he turned to Joe White. Andy works for Joe at Kanakuk Kamps, so he asked for thirty minutes of Joe's time to discuss the situation.

What Joe shared with Andy inspired me so much that I thought about it nonstop for days. Andy left encouraged and told Stephanie about it, and she shared it with me.

"Character is developed on the bench," Joe told Andy. In other words, this football season Sam is receiving one of the best lessons of his life, a lesson that will probably go with him through the rest of his life. A few weeks into the season, Sam was asked to take the top spot. He declined. It was more important to Sam to continue with the team he started the season with—the second-string team. That a boy, Sam! He has a very bright future ahead of him.

What is more important to you? Winning, succeeding, or developing character? Sam chose character.

The ROI Parent

My friend Michael Hall taught me the term ROI years ago, and it simply means "return on investment." Investopedia.com defines ROI as "a performance measure used to evaluate the efficiency of an investment or to compare the efficiency of a number of different investments."[7]

Michael is a business guru and a committed follower of Jesus. We banter back and forth on this term and its application in the church, even though it's hard for me to look at ministries and people as investments. It is even harder for me to look at my children as an investment.

My daughter loves dance. She takes dance classes every week and has for five years. She's in a group with twelve other girls who are equally passionate about the arts. We are good friends with the teachers and many of the parents.

Last year the girls competed as a team at several events in our area. Seeing thirteen girls dressed up like little farmers singing "A Bushel and Peck" is precious—the best I've ever seen. Did you catch that? I admit it … that was a trophy parent moment. Anyway, they all have their places in the choreography. The song is set for all thirteen girls, and it's obvious when one is missing.

So Corynn, Amy, and I have five years and thousands of dollars invested in dance. Even Carson, her little brother, has time invested because he has played Legos for hours in the lobby of the dance studio. So imagine our shock and disappointment when Corynn lit up at Carson's tae kwon do class the other night.

"Mom, I think I would rather be in karate," Corynn said.

"What?!" Amy responded in utter shock. She beat me to the response.

"It sure would be fun if Carson and I could do this together. Besides, I'm here watching, so I might as well be in the class," Corynn explained.

Several thoughts came to my mind.

She is eight. Started dance when she was three. Most Olympic athletes start training around three. She is locked into dance and could possibly turn professional. She could be on a Branson stage soon, saving money for college. She has what it takes to perform on Broadway. I see her headlining a show, therefore no tae kwon do.

We handled it like experts and simply stopped taking her to Carson's class.

Actually, I say that in jest.

When I saw that we would receive a family discount for both kids in karate, it was hard for me to prohibit Corynn from participating. Her desire for karate eventually subsided, and she remains in dance class to this day. *Her choice, not ours.* She will one day develop other interests, and that is okay—and should be encouraged. Childhood is not the time to lock into one activity. Childhood is the time to explore.

My parents allowed me to pursue different hobbies and activities. At age ten, I expressed interest in learning my dad's hobby. I grew up listening to him on a daily basis saying, "Whiskey - Nine -

Mexico - America - Foxtrot, W9MAF," which are the call letters of his passion in life, ham radio. He received his amateur radio operator's license at the age of twelve. After fifty years, he still connects daily with people all over the world.

He supported my initial interest and bought me the necessary books to study for the entry-level exam. Level-one ham radio is exclusively speaking in Morse Code. At this level, speaking on air is forbidden, so I studied those dots and dashes for weeks. One weekend my dad decided to test me. I sat on the floor next to his desk as he started on the clicker. He slowly progressed through the alphabet, and I kept up.

Within five minutes I came to the realization, *I hate this!*

I remember thinking to myself, *How am I going to break this to Dad? This is his passion. He will be so disappointed in me. I can't see myself doing this every day after school. It's just not my thing.*

"Dad, I don't think I want to do ham radio," I said and waited for his reaction.

There was no reaction or rejection. No "give it more time" or a "you are just starting; you'll eventually like it." He supported my decision.

My dad is an engineer. I am not. There was great wisdom in the way my dad let me walk away from ham radio. He saw it in my eyes. Instead, I pursued my grandfather's passion of photography. The first time I stepped into a darkroom with Grandpa Cunningham, I was hooked. Photography was my passion for twelve years before the Lord called me into ministry.

I am so thankful for parents who did not lock me into a single sport or activity. They let me explore and discover on my own.

I thank them for many things, but while writing this book I realized how important that truly is for children. Thanks, Mom and Dad.

When is it okay to walk away from a sport, instrument, activity, or hobby? Jonathan Hill, my friend, a member of Woodland Hills Family Church, and a Branson entertainer, has parents who continually reevaluated his position in sports.

His parents raised him and his brother to be competitive in a healthy way. Josh and Jonathan competed on a US swim team from seven years old until high school graduation. After high school, Josh swam competitively for a Big 12 school, but Jonathan turned to performance on the stage. Every year as children, Jonathan and Josh enjoyed a two-week break from swimming just before school started up in August. Their mom sat them down, looked them in the eyes, and asked, "Do you want to commit to swimming for another year?" They would answer, "Yes," and get up to go about their day. Not enough for Mom. She sat them back down and asked again, "Do you *really* want to continue swimming this year? Because if you say yes, you are committed to this for a whole year. There is no quitting halfway through."

On those cold, dark January mornings around 5:00 a.m. when Jonathan and Josh ignored the alarm clock and slept in, their mom had none of it. There was no complaining allowed. Their mom took a fair and balanced approach to investment, commitment, and individual discovery.

Gifted, Companion, and Rescue

One of my colleagues in ministry served for a number of years as the clinical director for a large residential care facility for troubled teens.

He led a staff of counselors who mentored teens daily, and he also made the final decision on the "intake."

Intake is a term describing the process of interviewing parents, assessing the risk of a particular teen, and ultimately receiving a teen into the facility's one-year program. This was not an easy process and required gut-wrenching conversations with parents.

Part of my research for this book included one-on-one interviews with my friend. The reason I chose to interview him was because of a statement he made to me after I told him about this project.

"Ted, about half of our intakes involve some sort of trophy parent," he said. "In many conversations with parents there was some sort of statement like, 'He or she is a good kid; they just fell into the wrong crowd.'"

My friend has a systems approach in working with these teens. The program looks at the home environment, not at the child alone, and the most effective counseling involves the entire family. When a parent understands his or her contribution and takes personal responsibility, half the battle is won.

In the thick of crisis, parents will say just about anything to get the ball rolling. They agree to counseling and help try to identify blind spots after the crisis first hits, but they lose the sense of urgency once things calm down. Parents often say, "We know we must change our home," on the front end of crisis, but quickly turn to, "Things aren't that bad at home," once they start breathing again.

The following stories are examples from my colleague in ministry. For professional courtesy and to protect the identities of the teens and their parents, I have changed the names and a few inconsequential details.

The Gifted Parent

Jason—Sixteen Years Old

Jason was an only child and struggled with depression, defiance, and declining grades, and he lost about twenty-five pounds before entering the program. His parents were both engineers. Mom was overbearing, while Dad was reserved and quiet.

The day of the intake, he locked himself in the car to avoid admittance. His parents lied to him about the program, telling him they were going on vacation and checking out a boarding school on the way. Lying is never a good way to start a care or recovery program. They told him the truth as they pulled into the driveway of the facility.

Like many families, his parents quoted the familiar phrase: "Jason is really a good kid at heart." However, unlike many of the families the facility sees, his parents didn't play the "he just got into the wrong crowd" card. Rather, Jason was "an extremely special kid who is just very complex and having a difficult time dealing with his uniqueness." They also said something that my friend hears a lot: "We know he is a very intelligent and gifted student, but his grades have been dropping. He's not achieving to his level." This was important because trophy children usually have parents who refuse to see things objectively and therefore have to adapt reality to fit how they view their children.

His mother voiced her concern and reservation that they made the wrong decision by bringing him to the program. In her mind, Jason was not like the other kids in the program—he was a good kid. She was worried that the other boys in the house would have a negative influence on Jason.

The ensuing phone calls were difficult because Jason's mother never wanted to hear negative feedback about her son. She held onto her beliefs that Jason was "unique." She felt guilt-ridden about their decision for a long time, and she often made requests for Jason to receive special consideration. She didn't want the rules to apply to him. She had a hard time with her son's reports (even though my friend warned her of specific tactics students use to get released from the program). She believed the negative reports her son gave, like, "The food is awful," "The big brothers are mean," or "The staff is incompetent."

Jason's mom was unable to see her own contributions to the problems at hand, and she aggressively avoided personal responsibility on every phone consultation. Eventually, Jason's mom pulled him from the program prematurely—against my friend's better judgment. Jason played his mom masterfully and convinced her that he didn't belong there, and he promised to do better.

About a year later, she called my friend and asked him if they could readmit Jason to the program. Things were worse than before. She still couldn't bring herself to say that she had made a mistake by bringing her son home early from the program, but she felt that things had changed since then. The program was prepared to readmit Jason, but the directors insisted that he could not pick up where he had left off—he had to start over. She agreed in the first meeting but never brought her son back.

Parents elevate their children to gifted status for many reasons. The miracle child brought into the family through adoption or after years spent trying to conceive can lead parents to believe that God did something extra special with this child. Children from successful family lines are often seen as equally gifted or successful because of the family history.

But this perspective is flawed, because all children have equal value before God. Gifted never means more valuable or extra special. All children are special blessings from the Lord and have intrinsic value because God created them in His image.

The Companion Parent

The companion parent adds a twist to performance by placing high relational expectations on children. This plays out in one of four ways: First, it can happen in the home when the parent has a buddy to participate in sports and hobbies. Second, it happens in a home when a strained marriage pushes one parent or the other to give extra attention to the kids. Third, companion parents sometimes reside in single-parent homes when the child takes on the emotional burdens of a spouse. Fourth, it happens in the home of the single child when Mom and Dad step into the role of siblings rather than the role of parents.

Savonnah—Fifteen Years Old

Drugs, sex, alcohol, and defiance were on her application.

Savonnah's parents divorced five years before the intake. Her dad was a physician and a classic "Disney dad," which meant that he set no boundaries because he wanted to be the fun parent. Mom was much less successful in her career, and she was bitter about it. The divorce was ugly, and the court-assigned parenting plans met with resistance. The parents were the classic "use the kids against each other" example.

One of Savonnah's glaring burdens was that her mother elevated her to the position of best girlfriend. They acted like peers when they were together, and Mom voiced frustration when Savonnah decided to ignore or dismiss her authority.

Savonnah became a trophy child because of the guilt and neediness of her parents. Both parents felt guilty for the divorce and the ugly fighting she witnessed in their marriage. Mom was a very needy woman who used Savonnah as both best friend and therapist. Both parents avoided remarriage until Savonnah gave her blessing. Truth be told, she was forced to become the most mature person out of the three of them. Her dad lived the life of a spoiled, entitled college kid, and her mom remained emotionally unstable.

Savonnah was one of the few students who looked forward to the intake. She needed a break from her parents. She performed brilliantly and excelled through all phases of counseling. My friend only delayed her dismissal because he was uncomfortable with her home life—emotionally, she was safer in the program. One of Savonnah's biggest struggles was that she often tried to solve the other residents' problems, and the directors had to remind her that she was a resident and not a staff member.

Although every member of the family progressed nicely, there were several hiccups when Savonnah returned home. She found herself back in the same situation of parenting her parents—and they returned to elevating her status.

Every member of Savonnah's family had an addiction to therapy. They had seen the same therapist at home for years, and the woman loved to psychoanalyze them, but unfortunately it led to zero life change.

Savonnah's parents also put misplaced expectations on the parent-child relationship. As a result, Savonnah bounced back and forth between her dad's home and mom's home, depending on which one most suited her wants and desires. And unfortunately, her mom and dad both tended to demonize and blame each other for any problems that arose.

Children need the security and safety of their position as children. A home without parental leadership is like a country without a clear leader, and where there is no leadership, the home dies. There is great comfort when children know who is in charge and clear, firm, loving boundaries are set. Consistency brings peace.

The Rescue Parent

Matt—Sixteen Years Old

Extreme anger and some alcohol use were on his application.

Matt kicked out the backseat window when his parents disclosed the real destination of their trip. About forty miles from the program, they told Matt about the residential-care facility. He was livid. Parents receive the advice to be truthful with their children through every step and to use an escort service if necessary—but it's impossible to do a proper intake when the child is lured to the program through dishonesty and deceit. It happens often—primarily because some parents fear their children.

Matt was a "good kid, wrong crowd" intake. He was an only child, and his mother became infertile after Matt was born. His mother was one of the worst offenders when it came to rescuing her child: she actually did his homework for him. His parents also bought him a new car after he wrecked his first one driving recklessly. He was their golden boy. Indulged, entitled, and given far too much privilege and not nearly enough responsibility.

Immediately following their first phone call with Matt, my friend received a call from Matt's mom and dad with a laundry list of complaints. No matter how much my friend encouraged them to let Matt's problems be his, and not to fight his fights for him, they ignored the counsel.

When trophy parents finally allow consequences, they rarely enforce them all the way through. Matt's parents were no exception. They would ground him for a week, then end the punishment a day or two later, having weak stomachs for enforcing boundaries and discipline.

In the same way, Matt only lasted three months in the program before his parents pulled him out. They fell for his complaints about the people and the program and were absolutely convinced pulling him out was the right thing to do: they believed they were protecting their only child with this loving act and brushed off my friend's concern that they were rescuing Matt from his own choices.

Amanda—Fourteen Years Old

Her intake application read drugs, alcohol, and an active sex life.

The first thing that struck my friend about Amanda's intake application was the picture that her parents sent along with it. It was a professional modeling photo showing their young teenager in a fairly seductive pose. When she arrived at the program, it was like watching a rock star get out of the car. Her parents opened the door for her and treated her as if she were larger than life.

Her dad was an ordinary-looking guy, while Mom was unkempt and fragile. Their daughters were attractive. Their oldest daughter was a senior in high school, made good grades, and followed Christ, but Amanda went in a different direction. She chose a life of drugs and sex.

From the moment of the intake, my friend fought to keep Amanda in the program. Her parents looked for every reason to pull her, which was consistent with the way they had bailed her out and catered to her every request in the past.

Back to the modeling photo for a second—it turned out that Amanda wanted a career in modeling. She was attractive, but much too young to be modeling in the sensual way her picture portrayed. My friend went to task with her mom because she wanted to send Amanda some special bras to "enhance" her daughter's appearance. The mother even considered breast implants for her daughter but was waiting until later. Both parents took extreme pride in Amanda's beauty—much more than in their older daughter, and like most parents, they had a hard time seeing this favoritism. But they had Amanda on a high enough pedestal that she could pull their strings when she wanted them to dance to her tune.

Amanda was one of the more difficult students this program admitted. Within a few days of Amanda's intake, she went to the emergency room complaining of "phantom" stomach pains, fearing she was pregnant. My friend was reluctant to call her parents but was required by policy to inform them. When they got the call, they started booking flights. It took some convincing by the staff that the situation was under control. Amanda was later released from the hospital (not pregnant) with no diagnosis.

The bigger rescuer of the two parents was the dad, and Amanda played him like a fiddle. She played the part of "daddy's little girl" when she needed to in order to get something.

One day she came into my friend's office and told him that she had accepted Christ. He was skeptical (he's always skeptical), but he let her call her parents to tell them the good news. After she left, he encouraged the parents by saying, "This is not the end." She was not "all better now," and finishing the program was more important than ever, especially while she was still young in the faith and susceptible to falling back into her old life. Of course, they ignored my friend's counsel. They pulled her from the program early.

She ran away to Florida and now is the single mother of a baby girl.

These stories are gut wrenching. My heart goes out to both the parents and the children. But we can see that the root is the same in each story: misplaced and misunderstood value. Treating our children like trophies accomplishes the opposite of the desired goal. Rather than experiencing life, love, joy, responsibility, faith, and maturity, trophy children embrace privilege, irresponsibility, manipulation, anger, and disconnection.

This is totally unnecessary.

It doesn't matter if you have toddlers, tweens, or teens—there is hope. You can turn the parenting ship around at your house. Don't get panicky. Stay relaxed. The solution is not found in discipline strategies. The turnaround comes when you establish appropriate value and prioritize the relationships in your home properly.

Parent Gut Check
Vanity Parenting

- Have you ever disciplined your children to meet the expectations of someone watching?

- In what ways do you see your children as extensions of yourself?

Perfection Parenting

- Is the bar set too high in your home?
- What are some expectations that need to be lowered?

Competitive Parenting

- Can you think of two or three children you regularly compare to your kids?
- What is driving your need to compare your children to others?

ROI Parenting

- Do your children have the freedom to bow out of activities or sports they no longer enjoy?
- How do you define commitment to a sport or activity? Is it season to season? Year to year? Is it a commitment for life?

Gifted Parenting

- Do you see your child as extra special?
- Have you ever found yourself saying, "He's a good kid; he just fell in with the wrong crowd"?

Companion Parenting

- If married, do you have a stronger desire to bond with your spouse, stronger than your desire to bond with your kids? If not, what practical steps can you take to prioritize your marriage in the home?
- What, if any, emotional needs are you asking your children to meet for you? Quality time? Validation? Comfort?

Rescue Parenting

- Do you automatically side with your child when you get a call from a teacher or coach?
- Have you ever rescued your child too quickly before all lessons could be learned?

Chapter 3
Know Limits

I stress out easily. My family's oversized suitcase is a major point of stress, because when fully packed, it weighs over seventy pounds. American Airlines, like most airlines, requires all checked baggage to weigh in at less than fifty pounds, or they tag you with an additional fee.

Before a trip I actually weigh myself holding the suitcase on our bathroom scale, then subtract my weight from the total to see how close we are to fifty. On trip day, my anxiety peaks at the ticket counter. This process usually entails a stern look from the ticket agent. In her head I just know she's saying to herself, *Oh please, weigh more than fifty pounds so I can slap this orange "heavy" tag on it and charge this guy fifty bucks.*

With two hands on the handle and a nudge from my knee, I throw the bag on the scale next to the counter. We both look at the digital reader as it goes from 0.0 to 25.6 to 39.7 to 48.5 pounds and stops. After my salvation, wedding, and the birth of my children, there is no greater experience than getting a bag under weight by 1.5 pounds. Thank You, Jesus.

When that happens to you, what is your initial thought?

Oh good, I saved some money, or, *That's great, the baggage handlers have some much-needed relief on their job.*

Or maybe you think like I do?

Wahoo! That's fantastic! What else can I stuff in there?

Then I rummage through our carry-ons and gather an additional pound and a half. Nothing irritates the ticket agent more, but rules are rules.

We all have limits. You have limits. Your spouse has limits. Your children have limits. When our load exceeds our limit, we begin to get run down, fatigued, and stressed out. I've found that stress is a socially acceptable term for anger and frustration. Do you treat yourself, your spouse, or your kids like that oversized piece of luggage? I must admit that sometimes I do.

When I see that our family load is close to "fifty pounds," my first reaction is the same as my experience at the ticket counter—"we've got a pound and a half to play with"—as I look for additional relationships, activities, and sports to stuff into our lives.

My children have different limits than I do, and no one knows their limits better than I do. When they were toddlers, I knew when one of them was thirty seconds away from a meltdown. I know when my daughter pushes her brother's buttons and when he's about to pop. Trophy parenting often pushes these limits. One more activity, one more hour of practice, and one more game keep us filling that fifty-pound bag.

Picture your life and daily schedule like that oversized bag at the airport counter. Don't picture your kids' bags just yet. Picture your own. You set the schedule, and you determine the pace of your home. My point is this: whether your home is relaxed, frantic, scattered, or plain out of control is entirely up to you.

Are you running at a pace that is killing your family? Relief starts by understanding your limits and building in margin.

Know Your Limits

My friend Lance Witt leads a ministry called Replenish that works with pastors who burn out and the churches they lead, or led. He said something to me one day that I will never forget:

"Ted, almost every pastor I work with started in ministry with the right motives. It is not until they get on the church treadmill of ministries, budgets, and buildings that their motives get skewed and they start making bad decisions. In some cases, it leads to moral failure."

As a pastor, I know exactly what Lance is talking about. Bigger does not always mean better. Instead it usually means more work and tougher schedules.

I lead a medium-size church, and every year I receive *Outreach Magazine*'s "100 Largest and Fastest-Growing Churches in America" issue. Many of my friends have made that list. When I grabbed it this year, I said to my wife, "Oh good, one more list to help me feel like a failure."

She laughed. The bad motives that sometimes drive me as a parent, sometimes drive me as a pastor as well.

It's true in every area of life. We allow the quality of our lives to suffer for bigger, more impressive opportunities—but more usually means more difficult. Solomon put it this way: "As goods increase, so do those who consume them. And what benefit are they to the owner except to feast his eyes on them? The sleep of a laborer is sweet, whether he eats little or much, but the abundance of a rich man permits him no sleep" (Eccl. 5:11–12).

Knowing your limits means understanding a sane estimate of your limits. A great question to ask yourself is, "How well am I sleeping at night?" Solomon said the more you have, the more you have to care for, so if you lose sleep at night, it may be time to take some out of the bag. When you stop caring for yourself and neglect your limits, you start making bad choices. You start with good and loving motives, but in the end, exceeding your limits leads to pain, suffering, and even death.

You know the pace is out of control when you reach 48.5 pounds and it's impossible to manage your home and children. I have five limits that I keep track of on a regular basis: physical, emotional, relational, mental, and spiritual.

Physical limits are linked to sleep, rest, diet, and exercise. When I walk away from a meal with portion controls, I feel healthy. Thirty minutes on the treadmill charges me for the day because I know my metabolism is working when I'm in meetings. A good night's sleep is like taking ten pounds out of the bag. My body lets me know when I am hitting fifty pounds—because it starts shutting down. I literally get sick when I neglect my physical limit.

Emotional limits flow from my physical limits. When exhausted, I'm not a pleasant person to be around. I am a morning person. We make no major decisions after 9:00 p.m. If we break that rule, my emotions take over, and I start to make rash decisions. When I feel irritable, snippy, controlled, judged, or inadequate, I withdraw from people and become judgmental and sarcastic. Usually taking control of my physical limits helps to solve my emotional issues. One of my mentors teaches others to never make life decisions or solve conflicts while tired. Good advice.

Relational limits are tied to personality. My personality has a greater capacity for relationships than my wife's personality—everyone's relational capacity is different. I enjoy parties where I talk to half a dozen or so people about a variety of issues. My wife prefers sitting in the corner with one person, enjoying a conversation for hours. Our marriage and ministry are better off when I let my wife be herself. Forcing relationships, extra social gatherings, and expectations on her only crams her bag too full and sucks the life out of her.

Mental limits include the learning, studying, and stretching of our mind. I reached these limits often as a student in my college room late at night, unable to cram one more bulleted list in my brain for a test. As is the case with all other limits, each one of us has a different intellectual capacity. Nowadays, spending my mental capacity by writing books, preparing sermons, and teaching seminars affects the quality of my parenting and family life. This is the limit that distracts me more than exhausts me. My wife knows this limit in me better than anyone. My kids know when I reach this limit because they catch me talking to myself. You may think learning is unlimited, but this is not true. Even our brains need a rest at times.

Spiritual limits determine your connection with your heavenly Father and the depth of your walk with Jesus. When our pace outruns our soul, we burn out. Have you ever felt this way? You have reached your physical, emotional, relational, and mental limits and find yourself with no desire to read your Bible, pray, or participate in your church community. I hit my fifty-pound limit spiritually after I max out all of my other limits.

Trophy parenting exceeds all limits. You pay high dollars on additional activity fees, and constantly measuring and performing is draining—not just for the kids, but for the parents, too. Your kids run at a frantic pace because you run at a frantic pace.

We need margin.

Margin means giving yourself and your family room to breathe; margin is a reserve. We've all experienced driving on fumes, with little or no gas left in the tank—and then we pass the gas station. If we ignore the need to refuel, we pay the price later when we run out of gas and the car simply stops moving. Panic and anxiety set in, and we feel helpless. Maintaining margin in our lives means keeping fuel in the tank and refusing to run on fumes. With margin, we do not rush from one activity or sport to another.

Margin is the space between my load and my limit. As a young dad and pastor, I often allow my load to exceed my limit, saying yes to every request for counseling, every party, and every meal invite. It wasn't until a much older and wiser pastor asked me, "Who is holding a gun to your head?" that I woke up to how I was living. He taught me that if I don't get ahold of my schedule, someone else will. I am a much happier pastor, husband, and dad because I learned the big word: "No!"

We must take personal responsibility for the way we invest our time, the amount of margin we allow, and how we prioritize. We are responsible for our own loads, and we cannot trust our limits to another. Only you know your limit. You feel it when you are at 48.5

pounds and exhausted—you know when you hit the wall. You know when you need to get alone and re-center your mind, heart, and soul. No one knows you better than you. Your limit is what determines your necessary margin.

Living marginless is being twenty minutes late to gymnastics class because you were fifteen minutes late getting out of the store because you were ten minutes late picking up the kids from school because there was an unexpected traffic accident.

We all need margin and rest, and we go without it only because of our own arrogance. We think we have an unlimited supply of fuel and strength as if we're superheroes. It is impossible for you or me to create or produce love, because God is the only source of true love and power. He gives us His love to pour into others, and His power is not meant for storage but for delivery.

Since when did I start believing that I am bigger and stronger than God? He rested after creating the universe. After Jesus ministered to the crowds, He rested. He told the disciples, "Hey, let's break away from the pack; let's chill for a while. Let's reenergize, recoup, and rest our bodies and emotions. Let's take some downtime so we can be more effective when we come back to the ministry." Okay, that's my paraphrase of Mark 6:30–31, but you get the point.

God knew of our rebellion against margin and rest, so He commanded it: "Remember the Sabbath day by keeping it holy" (Ex. 20:8). Holy means set apart. We are not to treat the Sabbath like every other day of the week. It needs a different rhythm. "Six days you shall labor and do all your work" (v. 9). God said we should work and provide for our families for six days. He wants us to produce, and He gave us the Sabbath to make us *more* productive. "But the seventh day is a Sabbath to the LORD your God. On it you shall not do any work" (v. 10). You need to slow down the pace for yourself, your spouse, and your children and find rest and relaxation.

Sabbath does not mean a day off. It means a day of rest. Jesus said, "'The Sabbath was made for man, not man for the Sabbath'" (Mark 2:27). The Sabbath is a gift to us. Take it. Enjoy it.

The demands and expectations of others, including our own children, are the greatest time thief. As a pastor I admit that my own church is guilty of this. Woodland Hills is a family church, and one of the things we guard more than anything is family time. It is crazy to say we support the family and then ask people to be at the church four or five times a week. Here's the rub. Everything we ask our congregation to take part in involves great ministry opportunities. Feed the poor, attend a Bible study, serve the recovery program, and teach kids on Sunday morning—all great opportunities, but not opportunities you need to say yes to every week.

We say no to really good stuff all the time. Say no to the church, school, community group, and extended family if it means taking your bag down to forty pounds or less and creating more margin for you and your family. Saying no is your responsibility.

Know Their Physical Limits

We know that our kids need to go to bed early on a school night. We book flights, activities, and plan vacations around their sleep schedules. We know how much our kids need to eat to keep their energy up, and we know when to spray them to keep their skin from burning in the sun. Generally, parents know what their children need physically.

The ropes course at Kanakuk Family Kamp is intimidating, and the age limit for the course is six years old. No five-year-olds are allowed to attempt it. But my five-year-old had the stamina of a six-year-old—another trophy parent moment, I guess.

Last year at camp, I talked one of the counselors into making an exception for Carson. I refrained from the "my kid is special" plea but went with the "if we don't hold up any other family, can we do it?" plea.

He agreed to let us on the course.

Challenge one is easy. You lock in your carabineer, hold hands with your climbing partner, and walk up two split logs at a forty-five–degree angle. It takes about fifteen seconds. No sweat.

Challenge two is not as easy but requires minimal sweat. You hold hands, but this time you walk on a steel cable that is parallel to the ground. Most five-year-olds could cross the cable in less than a minute.

Challenge three is tricky. Crab crawling across a nylon net looks easy from the ground, but from ten feet up this challenge can be humbling. This was the first challenge on which I noticed the limitations of my five-year-old. The wood slats in the nylon net were designed for a person taller than forty-two inches. Carson was forty inches at the time. The difference sounds small, but when your feet miss the slat by two inches, it might as well be a foot.

Carson had a solution. He jumped on my back and asked me to carry him across. Realizing we had six challenges to go, I said no. It was physically impossible.

"Carson, you need to be strong, man up, and get across this net," I said. He looked at me as though I'd grounded him for a month.

What kind of father refuses to carry his son across a treacherous course? I call it tough love. Right there on the course, he shut down, and I watched his spirit leave the challenge.

Challenge four was the deal breaker. This ropes course features three levels, with three to four challenges on each level. This particular challenge included two ropes for each person, one to walk on and one over your head to hold onto. Again, the overhead rope was just out of reach for Carson. Halfway through this challenge, he teared up, stepped off the rope, and dangled on his support harness.

He was done.

Knowing good and well that he'd hit the fifty-pound mark, I implored him to continue and simply finish this challenge. His watery eyes turned to tears and flowed down his cheeks.

Did I mention we were on display? Other families and counselors watched how Ted Cunningham, the speaker for this camp term, cared for his son. Would he be tough? Would he understand? Would he carry his son to the finish line? The pressure was on.

It was at that moment that my father, Ron Cunningham, came out in me.

"Come on, Carson, you can do this!" I shouted under my breath. "Get back on the rope, Son, and have a good time!"

We finished level one, but that was it. Fortunately, they have a ladder that serves as a shortcut to the top level and zip line. We climbed the ladder and enjoyed the ride down to the bottom.

We throw margin out the window when on display. My son's capacity and limit are different from mine. Stretching our children at times is good for their character, but forcing their limits to match our limits provokes them to wrath and bitterness.

Know Their Emotional Limits

Your child's emotional capacity is directly linked to his or her physical capacity.

Remember my story from the last chapter of trying to impress Joe White with my parenting? One Sunday after church Joe and his wife, Debbie Jo, invited my family out to lunch, and honestly, it wasn't the best day for the Cunninghams. I had completed a marriage seminar on that Friday and Saturday and arrived home early enough to take the kids down to the lake for a late-night canoe ride. Saturday evening I studied for Sunday's message.

By Sunday afternoon, after church, I'm always ready for a nap. There's nothing better than grabbing lunch with the family, coming home, turning on NASCAR, and dozing off for an hour or so. I believe God is in the nap.

Even knowing that my entire family had reached our physical and emotional limits, I agreed anyway to join Joe and Debbie Jo for lunch. Oh, how I ignore the limits.

On the way out of the parking lot I noticed some new members to our church. Their two-year-old daughter was in need of a nap. She looked like she was only a few minutes away from a meltdown. That's what I love about babies and toddlers. When they need a nap, they have an automatic buzzer that goes off and lets you know.

I rolled up alongside our new friends and invited them to lunch. They accepted the invitation, and wouldn't you know it, their sweet little baby girl was a perfect angel. God gave her an extra measure of strength, and she enjoyed herself all the way through our extended lunch. Our kids and theirs got along great and made it through lunch incident-free. We were grateful. The entire time, I was a trophy parent, too concerned with what others thought. I had the same feelings and anxiety as that day on the canoe. Another lesson learned. No margin leads to trophy parent moments.

Leaving margin in life builds up our children. The next time you think that adding one more activity, event, or opportunity to the schedule will help your child, hit the Pause button. Downtime is the ticket to enjoying life as a family. It helps our children produce, recharge, find balance, and excel in their other activities.

Know Their Relational Limits

Socializing and building relationships is an important part of growing up. Spending time on the playground, in the sandbox, and at church is necessary for children to develop relationship and communication skills.

The Cunningham home is a safe place. We go to great lengths to maintain honor and safety in our home. That means speaking kind words, esteeming each other as highly valuable, and serving one another. We seek forgiveness when we offend one of the other family members and reconcile any unsettled issues before bed each night. We pray together as a family every night before bed. We take turns praying for each other, for grandmas and grandpas, and even for the kids' teachers. It's hard to go to bed angry or unsettled after time spent in prayer.

Our children attend public school, and so our children face opposition to our home's values and beliefs on a daily basis. We encourage this interaction because we want our children befriending kids who use foul language and spending time with kids whose parents are separated or divorced. I hope they love on the special-needs child in their class, and I pray that they approach the outcast on the playground.

If you homeschool your children, I honor and respect that, and if you disagree with our choice, that's fine. The debate over private school, Christian school, public school, or home school is silly—parents are responsible to make schooling choices for their own kids. Like beating a dead horse, we show signs of legalism when we take our personal approach and try to cram it down the throats of others.

I love picking up my children from school because our family time starts in the car. We call it "the debrief." No matter how hard the day was, our kids have our car time to look forward to. They know it's a safe place.

Knowing your child's relational limits starts by understanding that they are just like you and me. They need a reprieve from friends, classmates, teammates, teachers, and coaches.

Our kids light up when we head home for the night. Not because our home is extra fancy or because that is the depot for their toys. Most times when I hear a "Yay, we're going home," I know it is because they understand that at home they can kick back, relax, and enjoy a little alone time.

Know Their Mental Limits

What's with some teachers giving out two to three hours of homework each night? Seriously! Thank you, Mrs. Rosebrough and Ms. Ramer, for keeping the homework to a minimum! I love my kids' teachers for guarding our family time at home.

Do you remember school? One thing I remember is that we wasted so much time. I rode on the bus both ways to school and back, sat in study hall, and worked at recess if necessary to complete my homework. Part of the trophy parent craze, now and then, is overloading our children with learning. There, I said it—and most parents I know agree with me. When I share that line at conferences, it receives applause. *Thank You, Lord.*

Due to the nature of my ministry, I travel several times a month. Amy, Carson, and Corynn are road warriors, and I take them with me often.

Last spring, we received a warning letter from the school. It was a form letter that is automatically generated when your child hits twenty absences. When I read it, I felt like a good parent. *No kidding.* Our kids had missed no assignments and made good grades. I believe those days were a needed break from the school routine. Honestly, I value my children's hearts and souls more than their academic performance, and that's why I love taking them out of school for some family bonding on the road. I never regret for a moment the time we spend as just the four of us.

Gifted classes and accelerated reading programs should come with a warning label. A child with a higher IQ needs just as much rest as a child with a lower IQ. I'm all for changing the level of reading or offering advanced classes, but this shouldn't mean that kids spend double the amount of time working their brains every day, every week.

Know your children's mental limits, and allow them to play hooky every now and then. Avoid truancy and becoming a source of frustration to the teacher, but give them time to kick their brains into neutral once in a while.

Know Their Spiritual Limits

There's a difference between spiritual activities and a parent modeling his or her faith. The latter is more effective, while the former becomes draining if misunderstood. Our goal is not to have children draw near to Jesus with their lips while their hearts are far from Him (Matt. 15:8).

Church attendance was the driver in the early years of my faith. If the church gave certificates for perfect attendance, count us in. We won that prize. The Cunninghams attended Valley Baptist Church every Sunday morning, Sunday night, and Wednesday night. The church held revivals two or three times a year. We only missed these events for sickness or vacation. If you took vacation time, the pastor's instruction to us was clear: "Pull off the highway and find a church." We disobeyed that rule on every vacation.

Memorizing Scripture, attending church, serving the community, and practicing spiritual disciplines all have their limits. It is possible to overload on good things. One of the things I love about Woodland Hills is the limited amount of time our church family spends at the facility. It gives us more time at home as a family.

Ephesians 6:4 is the clearest instruction we have on this particular limit. Paul encouraged dads with, "Do not provoke your children to anger by the way you treat them. Rather, bring them up with the discipline and instruction that comes from the Lord" (NLT). I like Eugene Peterson's paraphrase of this verse in *The Message*: "Fathers, don't exasperate your children by coming down hard on them. Take them by the hand and lead them in the way of the Master."

I remember teaching Carson how to cross a busy street in Times Square by holding his hand. Corynn learned how to walk down a bumpy path to our favorite fishing hole by holding my hand. On the ropes course at Kanakuk Kamps every summer, we hold hands and build trust in each other. Children learn about God the same way.

Christian parents tend to force God down the throats of their children. The hand-holding illustration is a perfect reminder to teach our children a love for the Lord. Hold their hands!

Simple Strategies for Maintaining Margin

I am a bullet-list kind of guy. To start you on the path for building margin into your limits, here are a few strategies for you and your children:

- Drop one activity.
- Reduce the intensity of involvement with a current activity.
- Take a sabbatical from outside activity for a period of time.
- Eliminate television and other media from activities to increase family conversation.
- Fast from technology for a period of time.
- Add more meals together.
- Declare a special "family night."
- Schedule a vacation.
- Plan a family game or movie night.
- Create conversational spaces in your home free of television and media.
- Before you say yes, make sure everyone knows how much time is required for an activity. Will there be time to practice between lessons? Will homework suffer? How does it impact the entire family?

- If you find an empty space on the calendar, leave it alone.[1]

Saying no to activities and opportunities paves the way to a close-knit family. The saying "everything in moderation" is true—balance is key. Participate in more activities that are fun and acceptable for every family. Pace them. Children need relationships more than activity.

Tech-Free Drawer

We lower the stress in our home by regularly shutting down the technology. One of the best things to eradicate the performance mind-set in your home is to unplug the gadgets, televisions, games, and mobile devices. The tech-free drawer quickly and easily reduces stress and builds more margin into our lives. Technology and our constant plugged-in nature maxes out all five of our limits. Here is how it works.

Step one: Clear out a drawer in your laundry room or kitchen and label it "Tech Free." On the appointed day, invite every member of your home to bring every piece of technology they own and place it in the drawer. That includes every phone, iPod, iPad, Wii controller, TV remote, and mobile device.

Step two: Declare a time during which the entire family will leave everything in the drawer. At first, do not be shocked if your family stares at the drawer. This is a natural reaction. Thumbs may twitch out of habit. Blank stares will probably occur from boredom. One hour is a great unit of time with which to start. Sleep time does not count. I know some families who are up to multiple tech-free days a week. I guess I'm just not that spiritual.

Think about it. Our performance mind-set and trophy parenting often come from television, Facebook, and the Internet. We compare our bodies, friends, hobbies, and possessions. Unplugging decreases opportunities to compare and compete.

Step three: Do something during the tech-free time. Throw a dance party in your living room. In our home, a family dance party (even though it requires one piece of technology) does not violate the tech-free rules. We avoid legalism and make up the rules as we go along.

Kids need this time to play in creative ways to use their imaginations. Relaxed, unstructured playtime allows children to pursue a variety of hobbies, interests, and activities. They also need distraction-free time with Mom and Dad. Do crafts, shoot BB guns, jump on a trampoline, start a campfire, search for critters, take a walk, ride bikes, or visit a local historical site. This allows children time for self-discovery and time to create, snuggle with parents, read, do math, daydream, paint, build, and explore.

A Break from Facebook

The effects of social media on the mental and emotional health of parents can be detrimental. Has it caused more harm than good? Does it feed the trophy parent inside each of us?

Facebook sometimes fills that leftover margin in our day. We come home at night and rest physically, unwind emotionally, disconnect relationally, relax mentally, and recharge spiritually. Rather than taking out some of our excess weight and leaving ourselves that margin, we cram in the last 1.5 pounds by staying up late on our social-media outlets, comparing ourselves to others, connecting relationally, and stressing out over something clever to post.

With its over eight hundred million active monthly users, Facebook (along with Twitter, MySpace, Pinterest, and others) changed the landscape of how we share the happenings of our work, marriage, hobbies, and children.

The average user on Facebook has one hundred and thirty friends, is connected to eighty community pages, groups, and events, and creates ninety pieces of content each month.[2]

Twitter reached a billion tweets after three years, two months, and one day in business. Now, users send a billion tweets a week. Michael Jackson died June 25, 2009, and Twitter users tweeted 456 times per second. The average number of new Twitter accounts opened each day is four hundred and sixty thousand.[3]

Information about our kids was once shared over the phone, at the PTA meetings, at soccer practice, and at church. Now it is shared on various social-media portals almost minute by minute.

Social-media usage accounts for one out of every six minutes spent online. One study found that those who are most connected in the realm of social media tend to be more "prosocial" than other people; that is, they are more likely to others-focus, through things such as being involved in volunteering, giving directions, offering their seats in public places, and allowing others to borrow their possessions.[4]

The Customer Insight Group (CIG) at the *New York Times* conducted a study to examine why people share content online. They came up with these five broad categories: "to bring valuable and entertaining content to others"; "to define ourselves to others"; "to grow and nourish our relationships"; to gain self-fulfillment; and "to get out the word about causes or brands."[5]

Physically, Facebook and other social-media outlets can lead to exhaustion. We can easily find ourselves staying up later at night to scroll endless posts. I pastor young adults who check text messages and social-media updates on their way to the bathroom in the middle of the night. We interrupt our sleep with the compulsion to connect to others.

Emotionally, social media decreases empathy and disrupts moral development. Young peoples' emotional development is affected by so much rapid-fire information. Our emotions lag behind the speed of updates and posts. Emotions take time to process, and when we rush them it has implications on our morality. Also, we can't help but compare ourselves with the status updates of our friends—which is like women comparing themselves with supermodels in magazines. It's not real. People avoid posting their failures in relationships and jobs. They avoid updates that their children received a C on their math test or came in last in a competition.

Relationally, social-media sites allow users to define themselves in terms of religion, politics, education, work experience, causes, brands, games, music, television, books, and more. They also allow users to define themselves by posting pictures of their families and lives for others to view. However, online chats and texting can help us connect to like-minded or interesting people when we need time away.

Mentally, we all need to relax, free from the pressure of finding something clever to say. The CIG recruited participants to deprive themselves of all social-media culture for one week. Here are a couple of the responses from the participants:

> I have a hard time imagining how much more to-the-minute information can become. With Twitter, instant FB updates, e-mail updates, what would have been considered fast even five years ago is obsolete. Sharing information helps me do my job. I remember products and information sources better when I share them and am more likely to use them.[6]

We all need a break from work, but Facebook keeps us connected to work for more hours than necessary. Pick work up tomorrow when you get back to the office.

Spiritually, has social media replaced your relationship with God? Are you at your limit or flat-out addicted? An addiction is created by a person's need for more pleasurable feelings in his or her life. Addiction is a reaction to a habitual need to act in a way to relieve stress, emotional discomfort, or levels of sadness. Here are a few symptoms to see if you have an Internet or social-networking addiction:

- Your social-networking activities cause you to neglect your obligations such as housework, schoolwork, or your career.
- You hide the truth about how much time you're online.
- You lose track of time while engaged on social media.
- Your social-networking activities have caused negative issues at work or school, yet you continue regular interaction on social media.

- Updating your Facebook status (how you're feeling) replaces "talking it out" with friends or family.
- You are often sleepless, or avoid sleep regardless of fatigue, to spend time on social media.
- You create an enhanced online personality unrelated to your real person.
- You lie about relationships or children to encourage more interaction online with other users.
- You define yourself, or feel inflated or deeply saddened, by the number of friends or followers you have collected.[7]

Parent Gut Check

- Identify the limits of each of your children, keeping in mind that each child has a unique capacity.
- What are the priorities for your family—those things that you won't give up (i.e., family dinners, regular church attendance, family movie night, trips, etc.)?
- Should you put those prioritized events on the calendar first? What can you change so that this happens?
- What are you willing to give up so you have more time together?
- How many family meals do you want to eat at home each week?
- Will there be time for your family to play together?
- How important is it for your family to just relax and hang out?

- Are you all doing the things you want to be doing?
- Is there anything that your family could drop to free up more time for family interaction?

Chapter 4

Everything Jesus Said about Children and Parents

The crowds following Jesus grew large, and as more people heard His message, word began to spread. When Jesus was in town, Dad cut away from work, Mom grabbed the kids, and they all headed to meet the man who performed miracles and spoke as though He knew God personally.

His message was revolutionary—life changing to some and blasphemous to others. His teaching style was profound and simple. He made statements that startled listeners, such as, "You have heard it said, but I tell you." He went against the religious leaders and called them out for mishandling the Word of God and burdening people with unnecessary applications of Scripture.

His teachings about parents and children challenged culture. He avoided topics such as parenting styles, schooling, and discipline strategies. He went deeper than that. He covered values, leaving home, separation from parents, entrance into the kingdom of heaven, and the priority of a relationship with God over one's family.

The words of Jesus bring comfort, balance, and perspective to parents. He calls us to love and value our children while preparing them for a life of following Him.

Jesus Valued Children

Does the heading in your Bible over Mark 10:13–16 read, "Jesus Welcomed Children"? I think a better heading is "Jesus Valued Children." In Greco-Roman culture at the time of Jesus, children were devalued, and childhood was almost an insignificant phase of life. That culture valued boys more than girls because, once grown, they provided for their family. But Jesus challenged that thinking.

The "seen, not heard" parenting style is thousands of years old. However, Hebrew dads raised children to be part of a bigger family: God's family. The Hebrew people, counter to the Greco-Roman culture they found themselves in, placed high value on children. Continuing this countercultural value, Jesus made a significant statement in Mark 10:13–16:

> People were bringing little children to Jesus to have
> him touch them, but the disciples rebuked them.
> When Jesus saw this, he was indignant. He said to
> them, "Let the little children come to me, and do
> not hinder them, for the kingdom of God belongs
> to such as these. I tell you the truth, anyone who
> will not receive the kingdom of God like a little

child will never enter it." And he took the children
in his arms, put his hands on them and blessed
them.

He was indignant. I love that. Many of the pictures of Christ
that we see hanging in Christian bookstores depict this scene with a
smiling, happy Jesus. *Indignant* in this text means "sorely displeased."
Jesus was downright mad at His disciples; He grew angry when
people devalued children. When the disciples kept the kids from
"bothering" Jesus, Jesus's followers received a sharp rebuke from their
Master.

Trophy parenting misplaces a child's value, but Jesus taught us to
value children in appropriate and healthy ways.

Woodland Hills Family Church meets in a purple castle at an
abandoned theme park. We love it because it's an inviting environment for children. Adults drive up and see the castle and think,
I hope they are able to afford a real building soon.

Kids approach the building and say, "Cooooool!"

Our campus is unique. You turn right at the old Roy Rogers-
Dale Evans Museum and directly into our parking lot. On the right
you have a massive wooden roller coaster, and on the left is our castle.

One of the things I love about our campus is that the adult worship center is in the back. To get there, you must go through the
children's ministry area. Critter Street for preschoolers sits on the
left, and Wild Woods for elementary students stands on the right.
Every person who enters our church walks right down the middle of
it all, and the energy pouring out of those areas is contagious. We like
our aging seniors to feel a little bit of that youth and fervor.

Everything about our facility, staff, budgets, and congregation screams children. We love kids, and we love connecting kids to their parents because we want them to know their value and understand that their value comes from the Lord.

To give someone or something honor means to esteem that person or thing as highly valuable. Children have high value, and their value comes from the Lord and is rooted in Him. Ultimately, they are to give honor back to the Lord.

At a recent marriage conference in Louisiana, the senior pastor of the church called me into his office to discuss ways to honor marriage in his church. The pastor had started at this church thirty-three years prior as the youth pastor. He served in that position for sixteen years before he became the associate pastor. After eight years as an associate he accepted the role of senior pastor. He shared wisdom with me in that short meeting: "Ted, I wonder if the way we do children and youth ministry in the church today is working against our marriages. We separate kids from parents the moment they walk in and entertain the kids while they're here. I think there are some changes needed."

I agree.

We strive for cutting-edge children's ministry at Woodland Hills. The struggle before us is to equip children to love, serve, and find their value in the Lord, not consume the church. I want my children to know where their value comes from and that their value is not based on their parents, their family name, what they do, how well they compete, their looks, their IQ, or their relationships. Their value is in Jesus. Everything we do in programs at the church points to that value.

I regularly ask my children, "What are the three most important things in life?"

Corynn and Carson both answer, "Honor God, honor others, honor God's creation." Amen.

The Three Lessons

I loved my days at Dallas Seminary, studying under gifted and passionate scholars. They taught me deep and rich truths as we systematically worked through all sixty-six books of the Bible. There is one lesson that sticks out above the rest. I remind myself daily of a truth from Dr. Mark Bailey's hermeneutics class. He said, "The two biggest mistakes we make when studying the Bible are not seeing enough and seeing too much." In other words, some people breeze through Scripture, observe little, and barely mine the nuggets, while others overinterpret and apply poorly. I am guilty of not seeing enough from Matthew 7:9–11.

> Which of you, if his son asks for bread, will give him a stone? Or if he asks for a fish, will give him a snake? If you, then, though you are evil, know how to give good gifts to your children, how much more will your Father in heaven give good gifts to those who ask him!

As I look back on sermons I heard growing up, this text was applied only to prayer. The preachers gave no deeper interpretation. But this verse, in the context of prayer, has many lessons for children and parents. I'd like to focus on three valuable lessons Jesus taught in this text.

Parents Provide for Children

The first and primary way we show value is by providing, and there are essentially two ways that parents provide for their children. They provide for the physical needs of their kids, and they protect them from harm. Parents have an innate impulse to care for their kids. I regularly remind myself of this priority in parenting. However, despite our impulse to care for our kids, giving our children everything they want is *not* the priority. When it comes to dinnertime, we give them what they need. Food is a good gift, according to Jesus, and when our kids eat, they are blessed. That's why we say a blessing before we eat—we thank the Lord for what He provides.

Think about the parent in a third-world country with the same innate parenting impulse that you have, but with very little means of providing for that need. My good friends Roger and Kari Gibson are two of the most inspiring people I know. They are on a journey with their family to care for orphans around the world. Their journey led them to baby Zoie, their adopted daughter from Ethiopia. She is our little African princess. Today, most of Roger and Kari's orphan care is centered in that impoverished and beautiful country.

The other day Roger showed me some pictures from his recent trip to Ethiopia, where he visited the Korah dump. The word *dump* is gracious for the horror I saw in these pictures. This dump started out as the place where the king banished the lepers from the populated areas. The land quickly became undesirable and eventually a place where the people dumped their trash. Unfortunately, the trash represented "survival" for the poor, sick, widows, and orphans. According to Roger, the smell is unbearable, and I can attest that the views are disgusting. Yet many kids call this place home. Roger watched children and moms picking things up off the soupy, muddy dump and putting them into their mouths to eat. These people really are the least of the least in Ethiopia.

Roger showed me one picture of a mother with a three-year-old strapped to her back. The mother had a sickle-like tool in her hand, which she used to overturn and pick through the filth and trash. When she found anything that resembled nutrition, she handed it back to her son. The picture I saw was of this little boy with his head tilted back as he licked his fingers. *Father, I pray for that family today and ask that they find a nutritious meal tonight so that precious little boy can sleep on a full stomach.*

Let's just sit in that for a second. That mom has the same innate impulse to provide for her children that I do. It behooves us to teach our children that food is a good gift. Let us receive our food today with thanksgiving. Parents and children need to be reminded and be grateful for this simple truth.

Parents Aren't Perfect

The second lesson from Matthew 7 is that we are sinful parents. We are flawed because of sin. If you are a guilt-prone parent, you need to meditate this week on these words of your Savior: "Though you are evil," which could be the strongest statement Jesus made against trophy parenting.

Say these words: "I am evil." You are simply repeating the Savior, and you can say it a different way: "I make mistakes." "I am not perfect." "I am marred by sin." "By one man sin entered into the world and was passed onto all men, including me."

A guy told me this week, "One of my favorite messages you give is when you tell adult children to leave their parents alone: get off Mom and Dad's back. Forgive them. They are not perfect."

Adult children need to understand that their parents were and are sinful. Forgive them for past mistakes. We all have a sin nature, which means we are going to make mistakes and say and do things that we regret. Learn to seek forgiveness from God and others and let your parents off the hook.

My wife got in the mood for some redecorating around our home a few weeks ago. We moved all the furniture around, and now we have an empty living room that is our makeshift dance studio. Each night our kids perform variety shows for their mom and me. They love the empty room, and they hope we keep it empty for a long time to come.

The other night Corynn came to me and said, "Dad, we want to do a show tonight."

My first question was, "How many songs?"

Honestly, in my heart at the time, I was thinking, *How many of them do I have to endure?*

She said, "I don't know—maybe like five."

"Could we do two?" I asked.

She knew my mind was in a different place, and my response closed her spirit.

As I tucked her into bed that night I apologized and said, "Corynn, your dad is wicked. Do you understand that? Do you understand that sin flawed your father just like it flawed you? Do you realize that, on this side of heaven, we deal with this thing called sin? Jesus delivered us from the penalty of sin, which is death. But, Corynn, your dad makes a lot of mistakes; do you understand?"

As I mentioned earlier, in our family devotional time we often discuss Proverbs 26:11: "As a dog returns to its vomit, so a fool repeats his folly." A fool repeats his mistakes, but a wise person learns from his mistakes. We all make mistakes—the real issue is whether we will learn from them. So as a family, we understand the doctrine of sin.

"Corynn, would you forgive me?" I asked her that night. She did.

Where is your level of forgiveness? Are you seeking forgiveness from your own children, forgiveness that you refuse to extend to your parents? You need to forgive your mom and dad. Give them a call today and thank them for giving you bread and not a snake. "Dad, I asked for food, and you gave me Oscar Meyer. Thank you!"

Parents in Light of God's Love

The third thing Jesus shared in Matthew 7:9–11 is a simple but important reminder: our parenting will never equal God's. Jesus said, "How much more will your Father in heaven give good gifts?" God values and cares for His children. Good parents do the same. No one cares for our children more than God does because He is the perfect daddy. He is our model.

Children Leave Home

Parents should have a glue-like bond with each other, not with their children. Misunderstanding the parent-child bond destroys marriages, creates entitlement in children, and prolongs adolescence.

William Wallace in the film *Braveheart* is one of my all-time favorite movie characters. My favorite scene is where he's all decked out with the blue face paint just prior to a sprawling battle.

Galloping on his horse, William Wallace (aka Mel Gibson) shouts, "Sons of Scotland ... will you fight?"

My favorite line in the movie comes in that scene, and it's said by the twerpy fellow who yells out in a nasally voice, "We will run!"[1]

I love reenacting that scene at marriage and parenting conferences. My best impersonation of Mel Gibson portraying William Wallace sounds more like an angry leprechaun than a mighty Scottish warrior, but nonetheless I passionately ask parents the question, "*Will you run, or will you fight?*"

There is always someone in every crowd who responds with, "We will run!"

I then reply, "Run, and you will live, but you will live without your freedom!"

We need parents with courage to take back the home. Placing your child in the driver's seat and revolving the home around him or her does no good for the child, no good for your marriage, and no good for you. A proper understanding of the parent-child bond establishes order in the home, prepares your children for adulthood, and removes the guilt-based tendencies of trophy parenting.

In Genesis 2:24 we read, "For this reason a man will leave his father and mother and be united to his wife, and they will become one flesh." We understand that verse to be a marriage verse and often hear it quoted at weddings. However, God is not talking about Adam and Eve's marriage, because Adam and Eve had no parents. God is speaking of the marriages to come.

Jesus restated Genesis 2:24 in Matthew 19:5 and expanded on it in verse 6: "So they are no longer two, but one. Therefore what God has joined together, let man not separate."

God unites man and wife in a glue-like relationship, but check the Bible—He does not describe the parent-child relationship that way. God's plan for families stands in opposition to kid-centered marriages. And the reason is simple: kids grow up and leave, but you and your spouse unite for a lifetime. You are not united to your kids for a lifetime.

I love lying down at night and talking to my kids because some of our sweetest times are when we pray right before going to bed. Discovering what is in their hearts is my joy as a father. The younger the children, the easier it is to get into their hearts. As our kids get older, they establish walls around the heart. It's harder to get in, but not impossible.

Corynn tells me everything at night. One night we had a daddy-daughter heart-to-heart, and she shared with me that she planned to live in our house forever. As we stared through the dark at the pink and purple fluffy flowers hanging from her ceiling, I told her that she would not occupy this room forever.

"Mom will probably turn this into a reading room like my mom did with my room," I replied quickly. Corynn went silent. I was joking, but she didn't think it was funny.

"Dad, why can't I stay here?" she asked.

I responded, "Because Mom and Dad have a job to do, and part of that job is making sure you leave home one day. You'll one day be married with a family of your own and with your own house."

My friend and mentor Gary Smalley taught me years ago to picture a special future with my kids. So I asked Corynn, "What do you think your house will look like?"

"I don't know," she said hesitantly. Knowing her reluctance to answer the question flowed from a sad heart, I gave it a few minutes. This was a precious, teachable moment with my seven-year-old.

Her walls are pink and yellow, so I asked, "Corynn, do you think your husband will like pink and yellow?"

"Maybe," she said with a smile.

"I wonder what colors your husband will like?" I continued.

"Daddy, will it be okay to have our house next door to yours?" she asked.

I was done. Teaching time was over, and I enthusiastically answered her question with a hearty yes!

Some of my favorite calls as a pastor come from the mother who is frantic about her tween child. For ten years or so, they raised this perfect, compliant, and submissive little angel. Now, the wheels are falling off the bus, or so they think.

"Pastor, I don't understand her anymore," I hear often from parents, some in tears. "She wants to shop by herself. She has her own opinions and ideas. She does homework by herself. She likes to read, but I think she is spending too much time in her room. I need a crowbar to pry information out of her. What is going on?"

"So what exactly is the problem?" I ask.

"You don't see a problem with this behavior?" a mom will ask.

"Not really. Sounds to me like your daughter is becoming an adult," I respond.

"An adult?! She's only ten!" the mom says frantically.

Therein lies the problem. When our children display tendencies often reserved for adulthood, we freak out. We don't want them to become adults. We want to hold on to them and retain their childhood and innocence. We want to keep them from adulthood and delay growth.

Separation from Mom and Dad is normal and healthy. Allow your child the freedom to differentiate him- or herself and establish his or her identity. It is unavoidable. When our children are young, they are more attached to us, but as they grow older, they gain the skills to do more on their own. This is good!

Here's a crazy thought—when you observe an activity around the home with which your child no longer needs your assistance, celebrate it as a sign of effective parenting. You have done your job! Congratulations!

Differentiation and separation begin around ages ten to thirteen. You can spot it when you start to see or sense active and passive resistance. Active resistance is vocal and argumentative: "I already cleaned my room this week and don't feel like doing it again." Passive resistance is nonverbal and dismisses or delays on requests. Kids drag their feet when asked to clean the room.

Separation is part of social growth, differentiation is important for their personal identity and individuality, and opposition in its very nature creates autonomy. Like it or not, raising children to become adults means transitional rubs. It's normal. Separation requires a new set of expectations for creating a close-knit family.

And whether you like it or not, Jesus is the most important relationship in a child's life, not you. Theologically, every parent I know agrees with that statement. Who would argue that? But do we really live this?

In Matthew 10:34–39 Jesus gave some of the strongest (and most difficult) teaching of the New Testament:

> Do not suppose that I have come to bring peace to the earth. I did not come to bring peace, but a sword. For I have come to turn
> "a man against his father,
> a daughter against her mother,
> a daughter-in-law against her mother-in-law—
> a man's enemies will be the members of his own household."
> Anyone who loves his father or mother more than me is not worthy of me; anyone who loves his son or daughter more than me is not worthy of me; and anyone who does not take his cross and follow me is not worthy of me. Whoever finds his life will lose it, and whoever loses his life for my sake will find it.

On a recent national radio show, the host challenged me on my teaching people to prioritize the marriage relationship over the parent-child relationship in the home. One listener called me a "prophet of Baal." If you are new to the faith, please understand, that is a very bad thing. It's not good to be compared to a prophet of Baal—they were evil people who led others astray.

When I left the taping, I felt discouraged and frustrated because I didn't think I'd had enough time to get my heart across. The show had turned toxic, and I didn't understand exactly how it happened.

For days afterward I replayed the taping in my mind. Then it hit me.

What about the words of our Savior? I wonder if the listeners of that program would accept Jesus and His message if He spoke it today? I pictured Jesus sitting in the studio and fielding the question "Jesus, what is Your message for us today?"

He would reply, "Anyone who loves his father or mother more than Me is not worthy of Me; anyone who loves his son or daughter more than Me is not worthy of Me."

I love my kids! I love spending time with my kids. I love going on vacations with my kids. They are a blessing to me, but my job as a parent is to point them to Jesus, not attach them to me. We want our children to make this decision—we want them to follow Jesus.

How far are you willing to go with that? What if following Jesus sends them to a foreign land that is unsafe? What if following Jesus means that they will work for a ministry, making no money at all?

I had a dear friend in high school who radically gave his life to Jesus. He was a skilled athlete who was the star in just about every sport he played. His career was promising, and he had his choice of colleges and careers. When he accepted Jesus, everything about his life changed, but his dad was a military officer who did not walk with the Lord.

When my friend shared with his dad that ministry was his career focus, his dad said, "Son, you're not going to make any money doing that."

I have never forgotten that statement. So I imagine my kids sharing with me news of their radical commitment to Jesus.

"Dad, I am going to Fiji to rescue girls from the sex trade."

"Would you pray with me, Dad, before I leave tomorrow? You know I'm going to share the gospel in an Arab country, and that may mean I give my life."

"The kids in Ethiopia need food and water. I am going to work at a shelter there, feeding the children."

The smile and tears that come to my face as I write those statements rest on me with such peace and comfort. I want my children to radically follow their murdered Lord and Savior Jesus Christ.

My own parents prioritized Jesus.

On August 17, 1984, my mom wrote a letter to me. I'm not a real sentimental guy who holds on to keepsakes, but I kept her letter. On slightly yellowing notebook paper, her words are simple and straightforward:

How's mom's boy? Did you know I love you very much? Well, I do, and I am very glad you're my son.

You're such a little gentleman and always so polite. Don't ever change.

I pray the Lord will call you to be a preacher or a missionary, but no matter what He has planned for you, I am behind you all the way. So will Dad.

I also pray that the Lord will give you a wonderful Christian wife

to love and take care of. Always treat your wife the way you treat me.
I love being taken care of by my men.

I'm really proud of your hobby, too. I think you do very well. Keep
up the good work. Pictures make beautiful gifts.

Just remember you're my favorite ten-year-old.

I love you very much!!

Mom

Thank you, Mom and Dad, for releasing me to the Lord and prioritizing my relationship with Him. The fact that I know and walk with Jesus today is because I had a mom and dad who prioritized my relationship with Him.

I mentioned before the principle Gary Smalley teaches of picturing a special future for your children. This simple principle plants seeds of hope deep within their hearts. When those seeds sprout and take root is up to the Lord and to water and grow that hope. The power is in the seed, not the sower. My mom sowed seeds twenty-seven years ago that continue to take root today.

As a pastor I am asked three primary questions when it comes to children and their faith.

"Do you allow children in the service?"

"When can my child be baptized?"

"When can they take the Lord's Supper or Communion?"

On question 1, my answer is simple. "Yes!" We love children and babies in church, even ones that cry out loud. If it gets to a point where we are unable to hear ourselves talk or think, then I just say, "Please enjoy our mom's area in the back of the theater."

We have no age limit for our service. Every now and then I rate the service PG-13, which means the content is adult oriented. Even then, parents have the choice of whether their child participates. I am not the parent.

Questions 2 and 3 have the same answer: "You tell me." You are your children's pastor. Do they know the Lord? Have they made a decision to follow Jesus? Have you processed that decision with them? Do they understand that Jesus died and rose from the dead? Have they confessed with their mouths and believed in their hearts? You prod your kids and tell me.

You tell us when they are ready to be baptized. We don't have a required age in our bylaws. When they deny themselves, take up their cross, and follow Him, we will baptize them.

Children Teach Us How to Follow Jesus

In Matthew 18:2–4, Jesus "called a little child and had him stand among them. And he said: 'I tell you the truth, unless you change and become like little children, you will never enter the kingdom of heaven. Therefore, whoever humbles himself like this child is the greatest in the kingdom of heaven.'"

While the crowd looked toward Jesus, He grabbed a child and used him or her as a prop. Children have an eagerness to learn, openness, trust, and vulnerability. They are also dependent on their parents for much. Jesus said we have a lot to learn from the way a child follows Jesus.

Neither my wife nor I have the spiritual gift of evangelism. We share our faith because Jesus commanded us to (Matt. 28:19–20), and it takes us out of our comfort zone when we tell strangers, friends, or family members about Jesus. The fear of rejection is our number-one distractor.

I don't know if my children have the gift of evangelism, but boy, do they sure have the gumption to tell people about their relationship with Jesus. Their inhibitors and fears are currently absent.

Carson once told me, "Dad, I can't believe there are people who do not believe in God. That makes no sense. Why do they not like God?"

"Great question, Carson. Many people choose a different path than the one Jesus laid out for us," I answered.

Carson shares with perfect strangers about their need for God. That is exactly what Jesus was talking about. Children know the kingdom and point people toward it. I love Carson's approach and style for evangelism—it's simple and to the point.

"Do you know God?" he asks a stranger. Nine out of ten people answer that question with a yes. He goes further.

"And His Son, Jesus?" he prods.

At their slightest hesitation he responds with, "Well, I do, and I am going to be bapitized." I spelled that just like he says it. He adds the extra *i*.

Parent Gut Check

- Is Jesus the priority relationship in your home?
- How can seeing food as "good gifts" keep us from spoiling or entitling our kids?
- What strategies can we explore that would teach our children gratefulness for the basics or necessities of life?
- Do you struggle with guilt-prone parenting? What will it take to let yourself off the hook?

- How is your relationship with your parents? Have you let them off the hook?
- Even if they are no longer living, have you let them off the hook so you can go on with life and serving the Lord?

Chapter 5
Spiritual Journeys

All great change in America
begins at the dinner table.
—*Ronald Reagan*

My children are Chicago Cubs and Minnesota Vikings fans, and believe it or not, there's a good reason why they refuse to cheer for the Chicago Bears and Minnesota Twins. It stems from loyalty to their grandfathers.

I established earlier that I am not a sporty kind of guy. So when my daughter asked which baseball team was my favorite, my mind went back to Wrigley Field and the ivy-covered outfield walls, the chocolate malt cups with wooden spoons.

A couple of times a year my dad played hooky from work and took my brother and me to the game. We parked a few blocks away from Wrigley Field and walked past dozens of souvenir stands on the way into the stadium. We rarely made it to the gate without the purchase of a button, plastic hat, or a little wooden baseball bat.

I remember sitting in those seats off the first-base line and eating a hot dog. The hot-dog vendor passed the dog down the row but threw the ketchup and mustard packets as if he was a Major League pitcher. An inning or two later we enjoyed the snack of peanuts or Cracker Jacks. By the seventh-inning stretch, right before Harry Carey came out to sing "Take Me Out to the Ball Game," we got that chocolate malt cup. I usually spent the entire eighth and ninth innings scraping off chocolate shavings with that little wooden spoon.

On several occasions we made it an entire family outing. Our family, along with aunts, uncles, cousins, and Grandma loaded up and headed to the city for the game. One summer we rented a roof-top just past the right-field wall and hosted a family reunion.

My dad watches every Cubs game to this day. He is grateful for his DVR and follows his hometown team all season long.

"Daddy is a Chicago Cubs fan, sweetie," I told Corynn when she asked me which team I favored.

"Why?" she asked.

"Because we do it for Papa. I only watch the games when the Cubs are in the playoffs, which is why we rarely watch baseball," I said.

Why is Corynn not a Chicago Bears fan? Because her other grandpa, Papa Denny, is from Minnesota. She wants both grandpas to be happy with her team choices. For Papa Ron she roots for the Cubs and not the Twins. For Papa Denny she roots for the Vikings, not the Bears. And our family is at peace.

My point in telling you this story is that messages of the heart pass down from generation to generation. Parents write messages

every day on their child's heart. Our parents affect the way we celebrate holidays, drive cars, buy cars, attend church, give money, make
money, spend money, save money, raise children, enjoy hobbies, and
vote. Who you are today is in large part a reflection of the home you
grew up in.

How do we know this?

Jesus taught us that everything about you flows from your heart
(Luke 6:45). Solomon wrote that you must guard your heart because
that is where life is (Prov. 4:23). Your heart is the wellspring of life.
Whatever our children think about all day long, which is what you
might call meditation, eventually seeps into their hearts. Once something gets into the heart, it affects everything else—as all words and
actions flow from that place. Every word your child speaks or action
your child completes flows from the heart.

What are your children thinking about all day today? The answer
lies in what you say to them all day long, from morning until night.

Matt Gumm, our worship leader at Woodland Hills Family
Church and a Branson comedian, has a hilarious set of parentisms.
From the stage in Branson, he shares in less than ninety seconds fifty
things parents say. It always gets a laugh. Get on your auctioneer's
voice and read the following parentisms in the next ninety seconds:

> You better change your tune pretty quick. I mean it.
> Is that understood?
> Don't shake your head at me.
> I can hear your head rattle.
> Don't mumble.
> Don't huff at me.

You act as though the world owes you something.

You've got a chip on your shoulder.

You're not going anywhere looking like that.

You're crazy if you think you are.

If you think you are, just try me.

I don't know what's wrong with you.

I never saw a kid like you.

Other kids don't try stuff like that. I wasn't like
    that.

What kind of example do you think you are for
    your brothers and sisters?

Sit up straight. Don't slouch.

Would you like a spanking?

If you'd like a spanking, just tell me now. We'll get
    this thing over with.

You're cruisin' for a bruisin'!

I'm your father. As long as you live in my house,
    you'll do as I say.

You think the rules don't apply to you, but they
    do.

Are you blind? Watch what you're doing.

You walk around here like you're in a daze.

Something better change and change fast.

You're driving your mother to an early grave.

This is a family vacation. You're gonna have fun
    whether you like it or not.

Take some responsibility.

Pull your own weight.

Don't ask me for money.

Do you think I have a tree that grows money?

You better wake up, and I don't mean maybe.

Do you act this way when you're away from us?

We've given you everything we possibly could—
food on the table, a roof over your head, things
we didn't have when we were your age.

You treat us as if we don't exist.

That's no excuse—if he jumped off a cliff, would
you jump off a cliff too?

I'm not going to put up with this for another
minute.

Just try me.

Look at me when you're talking to me. Don't look
at me that way.

Don't make me say this again!

Are you going to apologize? Well, sorry just ain't
good enough.

You are going to church and you are going to
worship the Lord with a good attitude!

I don't care who started it, I am going to finish it!

We are at church, and everybody is going to act
like Christians.

Knock it off.

Don't slam the door.

Don't turn your back on me.

Wait until your father gets home.

If you had a brain, you'd be dangerous.

> If I've told you once, I've told you a thousand
>   times.
> Just because your finger fits in your nose does not mean
>   that is where it belongs.[1]

I have fifty of my own sayings that get said over and over in our house. Do you? The point is that we mold and shape the hearts of our children with our words. In the early years of their lives, my wife and I are the primary authors of our children's hearts. We write thousands and thousands of messages on our children's hearts throughout their childhood. Every day we speak words that brand their hearts. We form and fashion their worldview by the words that flow from our mouths and eventually seep into their hearts.

Deuteronomy 6:5–9 teaches that it is parents' primary responsibility to impress a love for God on their child's heart:

> Love the LORD your God with all your heart and with all your soul and with all your strength. These commandments that I give you today are to be upon your hearts. Impress them on your children. Talk about them when you sit at home and when you walk along the road, when you lie down and when you get up. Tie them as symbols on your hands and bind them on your foreheads. Write them on the doorframes of your houses and on your gates.

There are two ways parents teach a love for God: *modeling* and *instructing*. When we regularly immerse our children in conversation about who God is, His character, and His creation, we build an awareness of Him into who they are as people. When we model a love for Him we inspire a thirst in them. This passage teaches us to be diligent and repetitious. Moses taught the children of Israel to regularly write a love for the Lord on their children's hearts—so from the time you get up in the morning to the time you go to bed at night, carefully write these messages on your children's lives.

Church three times a week, vacation Bible school, Awana, and Christian camp every summer only go so far. What parents do at home with their children far outweighs all these other influences. When parents live disconnected in their behavior and beliefs, kids take notice. Your children's spiritual journeys will mimic yours because they have a front-row seat to your spiritual journey.

This past summer at Kanakuk Family Kamp a staunch fundamentalist Christian father lamented to the families that his tweens did not fear the Lord or desire to walk with Him. The context of the conversation was church attendance, discipline strategies, and Bible studies. Finally, one kind and loving pastor stood up and asked the perfect question.

"Are you overlooking the obvious?" he asked the father.

"What do you mean?" the dad asked.

"Do your kids have a relationship with Jesus?" the pastor asked with great humility.

The dad was silent. God changes the heart of a child, not parents. Our responsibility is to believe and possess what we want for our kids. You cannot give your child what you do not possess. These tweens follow their dad's example, and it's likely that he raised his kids to be just like him.

Parenting starts with your own spiritual journey, not your child's. Work on your own heart to give your children the model and instruction they need to know Jesus.

One of the dangers of plugging into your child and treating him or her as the source of life is that you remove God as your true Source. Remove all the false expectations that your child is here to meet your emotional and relational needs. Codependence is relying on your children to make or keep you happy. The codependent parent copes by blaming the child for his or her unhappiness. Every parent has a tendency toward codependence. It sounds like this:

"You make me mad."

"Knock it off—you are embarrassing me!"

Have you ever caught yourself saying one of those two phrases to a two-year-old? *I have*. How embarrassing to think of blaming my child for my emotions. My child is not responsible for my emotions. Here is the equation. I am 100 percent responsible for what I think and feel, and my child is 0 percent responsible for what I think and feel.

God is ultimately the One who meets our needs. He is the Source of all that we are and will be, and when we look to our child to meet our needs, we find disappointment. It's God's job to be the Source of life. Start every day with the truth that God loves you more than anyone else does or can and that He desires to give you more of His power and love. Cultivate a desire to know Him better today than you did yesterday.

Parents must be filled by God, because, as I said earlier, you cannot give to your children what you do not possess yourself: "We love because he first loved us" (1 John 4:19). It is only after I fill myself with God's love that I have something to give my spouse and children.

Don't expect your children to get along with other kids on the playground if you can't get along with your own spouse. Don't expect your children to forgive your mistakes if you are unwilling to forgive your own parents for their mistakes. Don't get mad at your child for stealing candy from the store if you cheat on your taxes.

Our children have a front-row seat to our spiritual journeys. They see and hear everything we do and say, and they monitor every word and action for alignment with what we say we believe. Do your behaviors match your beliefs?

Last night, Corynn asked me, "Dad, were you ever called a nerd in school?"

"Yes, many times," I said.

"How did that make you feel?" she asked.

"*Nerd* never bothered me. I carried a briefcase to kindergarten, so all the kids carrying a backpack thought I was strange. But Alex P. Keaton from *Family Ties* was my hero. I wanted to be like him, successful in school and business," I said.

"Well, I hope I never get called that name because I won't like it," she said.

At that moment, in my head, my parenting strategies began to focus on ways she could present herself to avoid the name-calling. *Wait a second!* I thought. *That's not what I believe at all. Why would I ask Corynn Mae Cunningham to become someone she is not to keep herself out of the name-calling racket?*

The answer is simple. When we allow others to be our source of life, we disconnect our behaviors from our beliefs. However, we know that what God, not others, thinks of us is the most important opinion. So I adjusted my answer to Corynn.

"Corynn, be yourself. Don't dress tomorrow a certain way to impress other kids. Dress in a way that you feel comfortable, beautiful, and modest. Don't retaliate if someone calls you a name. Remember, God is our Source of life. When you understand what God thinks of you, you will find pity in your heart for the insecurity flowing from the name-callers," I said.

Parents and children alone are incapable of creating security, love, power, and fulfillment. God gives us unlimited power and love, and our job is to stay connected to Him. He gives His grace, love, and power to the humble, not the proud. Humility is a lost virtue in most homes today. Marriages and families must start with James 4:6: "God opposes the proud but gives grace to the humble."

Imagine for a moment a blue plastic bucket that has a supply of clean, crystal-clear water from God. This water never runs out. Unlike the bucket, your child has limits and will eventually run out. Jesus told the woman who came with her bucket to the well that she would thirst again after the water in her bucket ran dry. Jesus promised that if she drank from the life He brought, she would never thirst again (John 4:4–14).

When you commit yourself to a vibrant relationship with God, you gain access to that blue bucket. You find yourself filled and refilled by God Himself day after day, hour after hour, minute by minute. You find yourself renewed and ready to be poured out to your spouse and children.

To teach our children to love God will all of their hearts, souls, minds, and strength, we must love God with all our hearts, souls, minds, and strength. This is the greatest commandment (Mark 12:29–30). I want it to be true of me because my purpose in life is a loving relationship with Him and with people. Without loving and enjoying God first, we have nothing of real value to pass on to our spouses, our kids, and our friends.

When Woodrow Wilson was president of Princeton University, he spoke these words to a parents' group:

> I get many letters from you parents about your children. You want to know why we people up here in Princeton can't make more out of them and do more for them. Let me tell you the reason we can't. It may shock you just a little, but I am not trying to be rude. The reason is that they are your sons, reared in your homes, blood of your blood, bone of your bone. They have absorbed the ideals of your homes. You have formed and fashioned them. They are your sons. In those malleable, moldable years of their lives you have forever left your imprint upon them.[2]

Parents who refuse to walk with God are teaching their children to live the same way. The strongest, deepest, and most transformative words our children ever hear are those of our own example. Children who live with parents who scream and shout tend to become screamers themselves. Children whose parents occasionally attend church grow up to follow that model. Parents who badmouth teachers and preachers tend to raise critical, cynical children. Parents who consume and avoid giving and saving money usually raise children who do the same.

In a Q & A session at a recent parenting conference, an irritated mom asked me, "What do you do with a teenage boy who is lazy? He enjoys his leisure time, has no desire to do schoolwork, and sits around all day."

"Get him a job," I said with no hesitation. Nothing fires me up more than a thirteen-year-old sitting around all summer, playing video games, and eating snacks. Get him working!

I continued: "What is he doing while you and his dad are busy around the house? Does he just sit there while you mow the lawn, pull weeds, and scrub floors, baseboards, and toilets?"

She did not respond right away.

My specific examples were intentional. In other words, *Hey, Mom and Dad, are you sitting around neglecting household chores? Maybe, just maybe, he is picking up some of his behavior from you.*

Howard Hendricks at Dallas Seminary once said this: "The church gets children one percent of their time in a given week. The school gets children 16 percent of the time. Mom and Dad and the home get children 83 percent of the time."[3]

Are you ready to turn your home upside down? Are you ready for a family of people who know and love Jesus with a deep, committed, and passionate love? Do you want your children to walk with Christ well after they leave your home?

There is something very simple you can do to plant seeds of faith in your child. The answer is family dinner at home and regular family devotions. Tim Clinton, president of the American Association of Christian Counselors, told me that having regular family meal times at home and knowing your child's teachers' names give you a 93 percent success rate in your discipline and parenting strategies. I believe it.

Family Dinner and Devos

Frequent family dinners can help your children resist temptation. According to a survey by the National Center on Addiction and Substance Abuse, teens who eat with their families between five and seven times a week are four times less likely to use alcohol, tobacco, or marijuana than teens who dined fewer than three times per week with their families.[4]

Creating opportunities to connect as a family drives your child's spiritual journey. Breakfast and dinner are important meals in the Cunningham home. Our kids rise early, get dressed, and meet Amy and me at the breakfast table before heading off to school. We discuss a wide range of topics, like kind words, hard work, respect for authority, world missions, and God's plan for each one of us. Dinnertime looks much the same.

Last year, Amy and I decided to step it up on our family devotional times. Instead of choosing another children's Bible, we decided to customize our own family time. We took the letters of the alphabet and matched them with an animal, object, or nature lesson from the Bible. For example, A is for Ant, B is for Bee, C is for Camel, D is for Dog, and so on. We went online and downloaded images to match all twenty-six letters of the alphabet. We assigned a Scripture verse and two-word main point for each letter. The A is for Ant and stands for Hard Work. Proverbs 6:6 says, "Go to the ant, you sluggard; consider its ways and be wise!"

Our excitement grew each night as we watched our kids memorize verses and grasp more and more teachings of the Bible. It turned into more of a Deuteronomy 6 discipline than we'd originally planned. Now we find ourselves talking about these creatures all day long.

Traveling across the Taneycomo Bridge near our home in Branson, I asked Carson, "Check out those eagles circling above us, buddy. What does the eagle teach us?"

Like a Mighty Morphin Power Ranger he yelled out, "Unlimited Power." Then we talked about Isaiah 40:31 and the power God gives to those who rest in Him.

Walking through the zoo, I noticed a bird handler holding an owl on her glove. I asked Corynn, "What does the owl teach us?"

"Never Alone," she replied. We talked about the owl as a solitary bird and how the psalmist felt alone, but through a confession of trust he rested in God's presence.

I believe in family devotional time with every ounce of my being. So much so, that I want you to see all twenty-six of these devotions that we created for our kids—A to Z. Start the conversation tonight!

Twenty-six Fun Family Devos
A-Ant

Go to the ant, you sluggard;
    consider its ways and be wise! (Prov. 6:6)

Main Point: Hard Work

Talk Time: The ant is a very busy insect. He works long hours. He also works as part of a team for the benefit of the whole community. We have much to learn from the ant's work ethic.

A sluggard is someone who is lazy and is often found sleeping on the job. Sluggards also tend to be complainers when assigned a task.

- When you are asked to do a job around the house that you don't want to do, would you say you act like a sluggard or an ant?
- Make some facial expressions and noises that would represent a sluggard or an ant.
- Name a few things we can do around the house that would show we are considering the ways of the ant.

B-Bee

> Kind words are like honey—
>
>> sweet to the soul and healthy to the body. (Prov. 16:24 NLT)

Main Point: Kind Words

Talk Time: Honey is good to eat. We want to use words that people find tasty, much like honey. Our words have the power of life and death. They can either tear people down or build people up. We have opportunities every day to use words that encourage our friends and family.

- Share one kind word about each member of your family.
- What is the opposite of kind words? Give an example or two.
- What kind words have you heard lately that really encouraged you?

- Who do we know that is discouraged or sad and could use some kind words from us?

C-Camel

> It is easier for a camel to go through the eye of a needle than for a rich man to enter the kingdom of God. (Matt. 19:24)

Main Point: Less Stuff

Talk Time: Going to heaven has nothing to do with how much money you have in the bank. Jesus taught us that money and stuff are not the most important things in life. He taught that if you want to be a part of God's kingdom (heaven), then you can't love anything more than God. It is really hard to love God with your whole heart when you can't stop thinking about all the stuff you want. You can't take stuff with you to heaven, so you shouldn't choose your stuff over a relationship with Jesus.

- What is more important, Jesus or stuff?
- Why do we tend to hold on to stuff?
- Are you ever tempted to love things like toys or games?
- What can we do to show Jesus we love Him more than stuff?

D-Dog

> As a dog returns to its vomit,
>   so a fool repeats his folly. (Prov. 26:11)

Main Point: Lessons Learned

Talk Time: A fool makes the same mistakes over and over again. A wise person learns from his or her mistakes. We all make mistakes. The real issue is whether we will learn from them.

- Can you share about a time when you really messed up?
- What can you learn from that mistake?
- What will you do to make sure that you do not repeat the same mistake?

E-Eagle

> But those who hope in the LORD
>   will renew their strength.
> They will soar on wings like eagles;
>   they will run and not grow weary,
>   they will walk and not be faint. (Isa. 40:31)

Main Point: Unlimited Power

Talk Time: God is our source of life—He keeps us going every day. We all get tired and need to be refreshed. When we plug into the Lord, we have unlimited power and strength. Next time you have a problem, go to God first instead of a parent or friend.

- Have you ever tried to plug into someone else as your source of life?
- Did they let you down?
- What are a few practical ways we can plug into God?

F-Fox

> Catch for us the foxes,
>   the little foxes
> that ruin the vineyards,
>   our vineyards that are in bloom.
>   (Song 2:15)

Main Point: Healthy Marriage

Talk Time: King Solomon described marriage as a vineyard. In time, a vineyard produces grapes, which can be used to produce fine wine. There is only one problem: foxes like to sneak in and nip the buds off the vines before they bloom and produce grapes. It does not take many foxes to wipe out a vineyard.

Marriages have foxes too. A fox is anything we allow into our homes that could destroy our marriages. Solomon said we have to be on guard and chase the foxes. A fox could be money, another person, anger, busyness, or lots of fighting.

- What are some other foxes that could destroy a marriage?
- What is one way we can chase the foxes away?
- Why is it important for kids to have a mom and dad who love and enjoy each other?

G-Gnat

> You blind guides! You strain out the gnat but swal-
> low a camel. (Matt. 23:24)

Main Point: Avoid Legalism

Talk Time: The Pharisees were a group of religious leaders in Jesus's day who talked to others a lot about how to follow God, but their hearts really didn't care about being right with God. They would make up their own rules and neglect some of the most important commands of God. For example, they would strain out the gnat, an unclean insect, from their drinking water. At the same time, they would not take care of their aging parents. They would choose which portions of Scripture they liked the most and obey the easy parts. Jesus really hated this kind of attitude. He used harsh words toward them. Legalism is when a person thinks his rules and ways of living are above what God commanded in the Bible.

- What is an example of a man-made rule?
- The Pharisees were leaders. How can leaders in the church today lead in a way God approves of?

H-Horse

> I saw heaven standing open and there before me was a white horse, whose rider was called Faithful and True. With justice he judges and makes war. (Rev. 19:11)

Main Point: Mighty Warrior

Talk Time: The first time Jesus came to earth He came as our Savior. He is going to come again. When Jesus returns, He will come as a mighty Warrior riding on a white horse. Evil on earth will come to an end. Jesus will lead all believers in a battle called Armageddon. It will be the last major war on earth. Satan will be bound for a thousand years, and Jesus will rule in His new kingdom. He will rule as a king! We will get to be right alongside Him as He rules.

- What will the earth be like with evil destroyed and Jesus ruling as king?
- How can we know for sure that we will be on Jesus's side in that final battle?

I-Insect

> I know every bird in the mountains, and the insects
> in the fields are mine. (Ps. 50:11 NIV 2011)

Main Point: God's Ownership

Talk Time: God owns everything. Psalm 50 is a wisdom psalm that paints a picture of who God is and what He requires. We sometimes forget that. This psalm is speaking to a group of people who felt God needed their obedience and offerings. Understand that God needs nothing. Offerings in Bible times were for the good of the people and showed their true hearts. Wisdom always remembers that humans need God. God already owns everything. We are not doing God any favors by bringing Him what is already His.

- If God owns everything, why does He require that we bring Him offerings?
- If God needs nothing, why does He desire a relationship with us?

- How can giving to others show them that we love Jesus?

J-Jewel

> Like a jewel ring in a pig's snout
>> is a beautiful woman who shows no discretion.
>> (Prov. 11:22)

Main Point: Modest Beauty
Talk Time: It is absolutely ridiculous to consider placing fine, expensive jewelry in the snout of a pig. The same is true of a woman who does not show discretion. Women can respect themselves by learning good manners, dressing modestly, and avoiding coarse language and nasty habits.

- How should a young lady care for her beauty?
- Why do you think some young girls act in unlovely ways?
- How can this family show modest beauty?

K-Knowledge

> But you must not eat from the tree of knowledge
> of good and evil, for when you eat from it you will
> certainly die. (Gen. 2:17)

Main Point: Obey God
Talk Time: God placed Adam and Eve in the garden of Eden to tend and watch over it. Everything God created was good, made for Adam

and Eve to enjoy. God gave them one rule: do not eat of the Tree of Knowledge of Good and Evil. The judgment from eating of the tree was death. Adam and Eve did not obey God.

- Why do you think we so easily overlook things that God gives us to enjoy and often pursue what He tells us to avoid?
- Why is obeying God important, even if we don't understand why He says no?

L-Lamb

> The next day, John saw Jesus coming toward him and said, "Look, the Lamb of God, who takes away the sin of the world!" (John 1:29)

Main Point: Perfect Sacrifice

Talk Time: In the Old Testament days, people would bring a perfect lamb into their home. They would feed and care for it. Then God would ask them to take the lamb to the high priest, who would kill the lamb on an altar as a sacrifice for their sins. There is a price for sin. When Jesus died on the cross, He paid the price and became the final sacrifice.

- How hard do you think it would have been to take a cute little lamb to be sacrificed on an altar?
- Has each person in this family asked Jesus to forgive their sins and become their perfect sacrifice?
- How can we best show Jesus that we are thankful for His sacrifice?

M-Mare

> I liken you, my darling, to a mare
>> harnessed to one of the chariots of Pharaoh.
>> (Song 1:9)

Main Point: Woman's Beauty

Talk Time: To compare a woman to a horse is never a good idea, at least not today. But when Solomon compared his soon-to-be wife to a horse, he was honoring her. When he likened his lover to the mare among Pharaoh's chariots, he was using an emotional word picture to tell her that she was the most important woman in his life. When Pharaoh showed up to battle in his chariot, a white mare pulled his chariot, while dark horses pulled all the other chariots. In making this comparison, Solomon said that his gal would stick out to him above all other women.

- What images can we use to praise the beauty of the women in this family?
- Why is it important for a woman to know she is beautiful?
- How can men best care for the beauty of women?

N-Naked

> The man and his wife were both naked, and they felt no shame. (Gen. 2:25)

Main Point: No Shame

Talk Time: In the beginning, Adam and Eve were in perfect relationship with God and each other. They roamed the garden naked.
There was no need to hide. When they sinned against God by eating of the forbidden fruit, they suddenly felt shame. They hid from
God and each other. Sin brings shame and guilt. Sin causes us to
hide.

- We know when we do something wrong because we immediately
  try to hide it from our parents and teachers. What are some ways
  you have hidden your sin from others?
- Is it possible to hide from God?
- The Bible says that when we try to hide our sin we will never
  succeed (Prov. 28:13). Whenever we sin we should confess our
  sins to God (1 John 1:9) and each other (James 5:16).
- Let's take time to confess before the Lord.

O-Owl

> I am like an owl in the desert,
>> like a little owl in a far-off wilderness.
> I lie awake,
>> lonely as a solitary bird on the roof. (Ps. 102:6–7
>> NLT)

Main Point: Never Alone

Talk Time: You will never see a flock of owls. They are solitary birds.
They spend a lot of time alone. We sometimes feel the exact same
way. The guy who wrote this psalm was crying out to the Lord for

rescue from his pain. His enemies were laughing at him. We've all been there when we feel alone and it seems like everyone is against us. But we are never alone. The Lord is always with us. We must cry out to Him for strength.

- Has anyone ever laughed at you and got others to laugh at you too?
- How did you feel when that happened?
- How does it encourage us to know that God is always with us even when we feel friendless?

P-Pig

> He longed to fill his stomach with the pods that the pigs were eating, but no one gave him anything.
> (Luke 15:16)

Main Point: Daddy's Child

Talk Time: Jesus taught a story of a man who had two sons. The father divided his estate and gave each boy a share. The younger son ran away and wasted all of his money on foolish, sinful living. So much so that he ended up sleeping with pigs, hoping to eat some of their slop. That's pretty low.

When he realized his foolish ways, he returned home. His dad was so thrilled that he threw a huge party. This made the older son mad. He felt his dad was showing special treatment. The father assured the older son that he was always with him and everything Dad owned belonged to him.

- This story makes us think. Should we celebrate when sinners find Jesus or continue to make them feel bad for their past mistakes?
- Do you ever feel like you are better than or deserve heaven more than another person?
- Have you ever had a mean heart toward someone who has come to know Jesus because you also know some of their sins?

Q-Quail

> He spread out a cloud as a covering,
>> and a fire to give light at night.
> They asked, and he brought them quail
>> and satisfied them with the bread of heaven.
> He opened the rock, and water gushed out;
>> like a river it flowed in the desert. (Ps. 105:39–41)

Main Point: God Provides

Talk Time: Have you heard the story of how God delivered His chosen people, the Jews, out of slavery in Egypt? This psalm is thanking God not only for doing that, but for also providing quail and water as the people of Israel wandered through the wilderness. It is really easy to forget that God takes great care of us and wants to meet our needs.

- Look back over the past few years. How has God provided for this family?
- How does He provide for us each day?
- Do we remember to thank God for providing for us?

- Do we have any needs that are not being met? If so, let's pray and ask the Lord to meet our needs.

R-Rainbow

> Whenever I bring clouds over the earth and the rainbow appears in the clouds, I will remember my covenant between me and you and all living creatures of every kind. Never again will the waters become a flood to destroy all life. (Gen. 9:14–15)

Main Point: God's Promise

Talk Time: In Noah's day, God destroyed the earth with a flood because of humanity's wickedness. After the flood, God promised that He would never again destroy all life on the earth with a flood. Every time we see a rainbow, we are reminded of the promise that God made and that He continues to keep.

- The Bible is full of God's promises to us. Why are promises important?
- What does the Bible say of a person who breaks his promise (Num. 30:2)?
- Can you think of another promise God has made and continues to keep?

S-Snake

> "You will not surely die," the serpent said to the woman. "For God knows that when you eat of it

your eyes will be opened, and you will be like God,

knowing good and evil." (Gen. 3:4–5)

Main Point: Satan's Lies

Talk Time: Remember the story of Adam and Eve? They ate of the tree from which God asked them not to eat. They thought that if they ate from the tree, they would know all that God knew. Satan told them three big lies, and they believed him! Satan still lies to people today. He wants people to forget God's words and believe these lies:

1. You will not die; you will live forever.
2. You can know everything.
3. You are in charge.

- What does it mean to be tempted?
- When do you feel the most tempted?
- How can we resist temptation (James 1:13–15)?
- Why does Satan want us to fall for his lies?

T-Tree

Blessed is the man

who does not walk in the counsel of the wicked

or stand in the way of sinners

or sit in the seat of mockers.

But his delight is in the law of the LORD,

and on his law he meditates day and night.

He is like a tree planted by streams of water,

which yields its fruit in season

and whose leaf does not wither.

Whatever he does prospers. (Ps. 1:1–3)

Main Point: God's Word

Talk Time: Trees need water to survive and grow. You and I are like the tree, and God's Word is like water. When we memorize and meditate on Bible verses, we are nourished and we grow. If we don't spend time in God's Word we will wither and die spiritually.

- Let's take a minute and each quote one of our favorite Bible verses.
- What happens to the person who spends no time in God's Word?
- What more can we do as a family to drink from God's Word throughout the day?
- How can we be "planted by streams of water"?

U-Unicorn

I warn everyone who hears the words of the prophecy of this book: If anyone adds anything to them, God will add to him the plagues described in this book. (Rev. 22:18)

Main Point: Biblical Ignorance

Talk Time: Sometimes people make things up. Things like, "Unicorns are real, and they are in the Bible!" There are no unicorns in the Bible.

There are two common mistakes we make when reading God's Word. First, we don't see enough. Second, we see things that aren't really there. We have to be careful readers of Scripture. When you read a story or verse from the Bible, ask yourself these questions:

1. For whom was the original message meant?

2. What was the main point the author/speaker was trying to make?

3. What unchanging truth can be put into action today?

- Why is it so important to carefully read Scripture?
- Why is it dangerous if you don't?
- Can you think of anything people have made up about the Bible?

V-Vulture

> The eye that mocks a father,
>   that scorns obedience to a mother,
> will be pecked out by the ravens of the valley,
>   will be eaten by the vultures. (Prov. 30:17)

Main Point: Respect Parents
Talk Time: Having your eyes pecked out by ravens and eaten by vultures is a word picture for death. Not listening to your parents, making fun of your dad, or treating your mom as a servant will cause you much pain as an adult. The Bible is very clear that we are supposed to honor our parents, even after we leave home (Exod.

20:12; Eph. 6:2–3). It is the first commandment with a promise. God gives us parents to prepare us for life in the world. When you listen to their instruction, it helps you throughout your entire life.

- What are some ways you can show Mom and Dad honor and respect this week?
- Can you think of something Mom or Dad told you not to do, but you did it anyway? What were the consequences of that decision?
- When you are an adult, what are some ways you can continue to honor your parents?

W-Wolves

> Go! I am sending you out like lambs among wolves.
> (Luke 10:3)

Main Point: The World
Talk Time: The world is corrupt, deadly, and decaying. Right before Jesus died, He prayed for all of His followers. He asked His heavenly Father not to take them out of the world. Instead, He wanted us to be salt and light to the world. Jesus is our Good Shepherd, and we are His sheep. We are to go into the world and preach the gospel, which is like sending lambs to the wolves. Telling people about Jesus is not easy, but it is what we are called to do.

- Has anyone ever made fun of you for following Jesus?
- Why does the world hate Jesus so much?

- If the world hated Jesus, do you think that His followers will be hated too?
- Who do you need to share your faith with this week?

X-Ox

> Without oxen a stable stays clean,
> but you need a strong ox for a large harvest.
> (Prov. 14:4 NLT)

Main Point: Dirty Work

Talk Time: The ant taught us hard work. The ox teaches us about dirty work. Farmers need the strength of the ox to plow the field. However, an ox is a large animal that makes a lot of manure. (Now would be a good time for everybody to chuckle.) If a farmer wants to get the fields plowed, he must be willing to shovel a little poop.

- What is the dirtiest job you have ever completed? How messy was it?
- What are some dirty jobs that need to get done around the house?
- What is keeping you from taking the initiative to get them done?

Y-Yoke

> Do not be yoked together with unbelievers. For
> what do righteousness and wickedness have in

common? Or what fellowship can light have with
darkness? (2 Cor. 6:14)

Main Point: Equally Yoked

Talk Time: In the Old Testament, God commanded that a donkey
and ox were not to be yoked together (Deut. 22:10). Yoking is when
the farmer harnesses two animals together to do a job. In ancient times,
it was forbidden to yoke a clean and an unclean animal together. The
apostle Paul used this imagery in the New Testament to teach that
believers and unbelievers should not be yoked together. We can have
unbelievers as friends, but not as partners. If a believer partners with
an unbeliever in marriage or business, there will be a constant struggle.

- What are some potential struggles of a spiritually mismatched
  marriage?
- Can you think of any problems that might happen if a Christian
  goes into business with a non-Christian?
- Why is it a bad idea for a Christian to date a non-Christian?

Z-Zebra

You are to bring into the ark two of all living creatures, male and female, to keep them alive with
you. (Gen. 6:19)

Main Point: God's Judgment

Talk Time: In the story of Noah, God got fed up with humanity's
wickedness and sent a flood to cover the earth. But before He sent

the rain, He called Noah to build an ark. Noah brought a male and female of every animal onto the ark so that the animals could reproduce. Even though God judged the wicked, He still took care of Noah's family because they obeyed Him. The animals we have today are here because Noah listened to God.

- What do you think life was like on an ark full of animals?
- Why did God choose Noah to build the ark (Gen. 6; Heb. 11:7)?
- Can you think of other times when God has shown grace?

These short devos are some of the richest times around the Cunningham dinner table. The best part is that they do not stay around our dinner table. The kids can have a rough day at school or make a big mistake on a test or the playground, and I take them to our devo cards and remind them of the dog returning to vomit. We all make mistakes, but our goal is not to make the same mistake over and over again. We want to learn from our mistakes. What a treat for parents to watch the seeds of faith sprout and take root in the hearts of our children.

Parent Gut Check

- Which of your professed beliefs do not have behavior to back them up?
- Where are you inconsistent in your walk with Christ?
- If your children explained to me your love for Jesus, what would they say?

Chapter 6
Kids Who Follow Jesus

God has only one love language.

A love language is simply the way we give and receive love. My wife's love languages, for example, are acts of service and quality time. Amy feels loved when I load the dishwasher, start the dryer, and make the bed. She loves her family and connects with her kids by going nonstop and serving us from sunrise to sunset. The absolute best way for the kids and me to connect with my wife is to serve her in the same way.

How do we connect our children to God? What is God's love language? Worship? Prayer? Singing? Reading His Word? All of these disciplines are good, but they are secondary to God's primary love language. Do we teach our children these spiritual disciplines, hoping our kids will connect with God once they leave home?

To answer that question, we must know how God gives and receives love. John 3:16 answers the question of how God shows love: "For God so loved the world that he gave his one and only

Son." God showed us love by giving us His Son, Jesus, to die for our sins.

Followers of Jesus know that God is the Author of our salvation. When you confess with your mouth and believe in your heart, you are saved (Rom. 10:9–10). We know what it means to receive love from God, but we offer many different answers to the question of how God receives love from us. Connecting with God has nothing to do with your preferences, personality, denominational practices, or doctrine. Connecting with God is not as mystical as we make it.

There is only one way we show God love—as I said, He has one love language. Jesus clearly identified His Father's love language when He said,

> Whoever has my commands and obeys them, he is the one who loves me. He who loves me will be loved by my Father, and I too will love him and show myself to him....
>
> If anyone loves me, he will obey my teaching. My Father will love him, and we will come to him and make our home with him. He who does not love me will not obey my teaching. These words you hear are not my own; they belong to the Father who sent me. (John 14:21, 23–24)

In short, Jesus is God's love language.

When we love Jesus and observe all that He taught, we show the Father love. When we love Jesus and keep His commands, we connect to the Father. Jesus did nothing without His Father. God sent Jesus, who received authority from His Father. If you want your children to know God, they must know Jesus intimately. Jesus said, "I am the way and the truth and the life. No one comes to the Father except through me" (John 14:6). That often-quoted verse usually comes in the context of an evangelism talk or a discussion of the exclusivity of Christ. We know salvation comes through Jesus, but so does our constant connection to our heavenly Daddy.

In John 14:7 Jesus added, "If you really knew me, you would know my Father as well." Catching the theme? Connecting our children to Jesus should be our chief goal as parents—after providing for our children's basic needs, we want them to know Jesus.

Years ago, a craze hit the church that resulted in everyone wearing bracelets, shirts, and hats bearing the letters *WWJD* (which stood for "What Would Jesus Do?"). Christians try to ask themselves this question in all of life's circumstances and whenever facing a major decision. The only problem with this question is we cannot say with certainty what Jesus would do in every situation. I think there is a much better question to ask and answer with certainty:

What did Jesus say?

To connect your children with God they must know Jesus. To know Jesus, they must know what He said.

Kids Who Are Connected to His Words

Some followers of Christ have no clue what Jesus taught. Years ago, a friend of mine called me right before his speaking engagement at a church and asked me, "Ted, where in the Bible did Jesus say, 'Fish for a man he eats for a day. Teach him to fish and he eats for a lifetime'?"

I had to let my friend down easy.

"Are you kidding me?" I asked him sarcastically.

He answered, "Seriously, I thought for sure He said that."

"I think that's a Chinese proverb," I responded.

He felt convinced Jesus said those words. I've heard many statements attributed to Jesus. Statements like "Forgive and forget," "Once saved, always saved," and "Worship the Lord your God on Sunday." Jesus never said any of those statements.

Jesus made many promises to those who abide in His Word. For starters, if you abide in His Word, God the Father, Son, and Holy Spirit are your constant companions, both with *and* within you. Also, you receive a level of peace and joy direct from God that is otherwise unattainable. You impact the lives of others in ways that can't be achieved by human effort alone. God will love you in a unique way. You witness miracles in your life that others can't explain. And you will experience freedom from that which holds you captive.

However, knowing the words of Jesus inside and out is not a guarantee of connection with the Father. There is a big difference between knowing Jesus and knowing things about Him. Some people study the Bible as an end in itself. Jesus warned about this thought process when He said, "You diligently study the Scriptures because you think that by them you possess eternal life. These are the Scriptures that testify about me, yet you refuse to come to me to have life" (John 5:39–40). Studying the Bible is not a guarantee of connection with the Father.

So how do we know if our kids have the words of Jesus in their hearts? Catch your kids acting like Jesus—if parents know the words of Jesus and act like Him, then their kids will see that lived out every day in the home. When we live this out every day, we pass on to the next generation the teachings of Christ.

Psalm 78 teaches us to remind our children and grandchildren of the Lord. The enthusiasm of this generation connects with the wisdom of past generations:

> O my people, hear my teaching;
>> listen to the words of my mouth.
> I will open my mouth in parables,
>> I will utter hidden things, things from of old—
> what we have heard and known,
>> what our fathers have told us.
> We will not hide them from their children;
>> we will tell the next generation
> the praiseworthy deeds of the LORD,
>> his power, and the wonders he has done.
>> (Ps. 78:1–4)

My buddy Dan Seaborn, one of the most inspiring marriage and family speakers that I know, leads a ministry to families called Winning at Home. He was recently highlighted on a broadcast of Focus on the Family. I listened to his talk on Psalm 78 on the way to the airport one Friday morning around 4:00 a.m.

Dan shared the story of his grandpa and how he built a foundation of faith for generations to come. Through tears, Dan said, "[Grandpa Jay] was my main teacher.... I don't always do this, but on this particular day I said, 'Lord, what would Grandpa do here?' ... Grandpa's passed on now. I remember the first Sunday

I preached—I used his Bible—first Sunday after he'd passed away. I did it not only to honor him, but it was the first time Grandpa had ever heard me preach because he's in heaven looking down, see.… He taught me a lot."[1]

To this day, Dan passes on his faith to his kids by celebrating when his children act like Jesus. Whether he is at home or traveling, the Seaborn family stops everything and celebrates when a member of the family demonstrates an action or behavior that exemplifies Jesus.

I know my kids are "getting it" when I catch them acting like Jesus. Here are some of my favorite words that come out of my children's mouths:

"Carson, you can go first."

"Sissy, Dad gave me this for my birthday, but you can play with it whenever you want."

"Corynn, did you have a good day at school?"

"Carson, I am so sorry you got hurt today."

"I'll break the candy bar in half, and you can choose first which piece you want."

"I'm sorry."

When that comes out unsolicited by Mom and Dad, I almost lose it. You know what I am talking about, don't you? When our children make statements that demonstrate an "others first" attitude of reconciliation, empathy, and sharing, we know that they are following the ways of Jesus.

Kids Who Obey His Words

My friend Steve Scott wrote a great book several years ago called *The Greatest Words Ever Spoken*. In this book, Steve organized every word

Jesus spoke into categories, and it's a wonderful resource that helps us observe everything Jesus commanded.

As a parent I know the joy that floods my soul when my kids listen to me the first time I ask them to do something. That joy grows when they listen and obey with good attitudes. Imagine the joy your heavenly Father feels when His children obey the teachings of Jesus. Remember, Jesus only spoke the words His Father gave Him to speak.

When I am on the other side of the house and I hear Amy say, "Hey, guys, it's time for dinner," there is only one appropriate response. Grumbling is unacceptable. When I hear whining, my voice is the next one my kids hear.

I ask the kids, "Did I just hear a grumble?"

They usually respond with, "Coming, Dad."

Nothing drains the energy out of my wife more than when she issues the same request four, five, or six times and it continues to fall on deaf ears. I have no problem being the heavy.

Connecting with God starts by knowing Jesus, then doing what He taught. The Great Commission places a priority on completely obeying everything Jesus said: "Therefore go and make disciples of all nations, baptizing them in the name of the Father and of the Son and of the Holy Spirit, and teaching them to obey everything I have commanded you. And surely I am with you always, to the very end of the age" (Matt. 28:19–20). Following Jesus means we teach our children to obey everything He commanded—but my struggle is prioritizing the words of Jesus above my own. Does anyone else out there struggle with making Jesus's words more important than their own?

"I grew up with Christian parents who taught me the difference between right and wrong." This is the most common answer

I get when I ask to hear someone's story—but the words of Jesus go beyond simply teaching good morals and values.

Our children need the words of the living Savior. It is how we connect them to their heavenly Father. To love Jesus, we simply do what He says.

Kids Who Value Jesus More Than Themselves

A few years ago, Amy and I thought God called us out of Branson to serve in Phoenix, Arizona. The pastor there is a great friend and leads a tremendous church. We put the opportunity before God and patiently waited to hear from Him.

For a year, we made monthly trips to Phoenix to teach at the church, meet with leaders, and even search for houses. My family accompanied me on every other trip. My kids loved the new friends they met in Arizona, and they enjoyed the house hunt. They had no idea that moving there was likely to be our next step.

Once we told them, my son had no problem with it—he was good to go. Corynn, six years old at the time, was against the move from the moment we told her.

"Corynn, what if we moved to Phoenix?" I asked her, standing in a home we were touring.

"No, I like Branson," she said.

"I like Branson too, but I think launching this marriage ministry is our next move as a family," I said.

"What about our church? We love Woodland Hills! All of our friends and the Pamas and Papas go there," she reminded me.

"It is very possible that we'll move here and move into a house just like this one," I said in an authoritative tone.

"I don't want to," she replied.

"What if God calls us here?" I asked.

"Okay, but only if God calls us here. I'm not coming if it is just you who wants us to move here," she said.

You may think that sounds disrespectful, but her reply comforted me. I want her more connected to Christ than to me. I want her to value the leading of the Lord in her life more than her comforts at home, school, and church.

Raising children who value Jesus more than themselves means we allow them to be uncomfortable and experience pain, trials, and difficulty at times so they can know and love Jesus more.

This is not the message the world gives us. To be honest with you, it's not a message that many parents give their kids today either. We teach our kids to value success and how to dream big. The question is, are those dreams rooted in Christ, or are they rooted in self-centeredness and self-glorification? We teach our kids to get as much out of this life as they possibly can, to go out there and make something of themselves. Mark 8:36 says, "What good is it for a man to gain the whole world, yet forfeit his soul?"

Corynn's soul is more important than her self-esteem, because Jesus wants Corynn to spend eternity with Him. We need to disown our tyrannical rule of self-centeredness, where it is all about us. We may place ourselves at the center of our lives, but it's not about us; it's about giving up our lives for the gospel and for others.

Kids Who Serve

Kids who know and follow Jesus understand that they are ministers called to serve. There is no better antidote to entitlement than serving. We must teach our children to seek out relationships and then seek to give to those people rather than to receive from them. For my son, it was simple and started early when I taught him how to open a door for other people in public.

Since most stores have two sets of double doors, teaching him was easy. I would get the first door, invite him through, and ask him to open the next door. We then waited for the Princess and Queen (Corynn and Mom) to pass through. I would high-five Carson on my way through.

He gets it, but he really got it when he held open the door for a rapper in Orlando, Florida.

While staying at an Orlando resort over spring break one year, my lessons on chivalry continued. As we walked out of the hotel to the pool, we met a posse of what looked like very important rappers. I am not stereotyping—okay, maybe just a little. Seriously though, if you meet a rapper like P. Diddy and he steps out of a black Suburban with eight armed guards, you spot him right away. No immersion in rap culture necessary. The hat with a perfectly straight bill tilted sideways, mega chains, a modest amount of tattoos, and all white clothes—he was a dead giveaway.

"Carson, quick, get the door," I said. I caught Carson off guard because he had swimming on the brain.

He held open the door, and the rapper was the first one through. He stopped, turned around, and looked at Carson for a second. Apparently, Carson had caught him off guard too. We had a special moment, because what happened next was unforgettable.

The guy reached into his pocket, pulled out a wad of cash, peeled off a twenty-dollar bill, handed it to my son, and said, "Here, kid, go buy yourself a T-shirt or something."

Carson's eyes were as big as saucers as he thought to himself, *These tall people carry lots of cash.*

The good thing about Orlando is that in this tourist town, twenty dollars buys about six T-shirts at any gas station. Reminding Carson to open doors is no longer necessary; now he just does it because the potential of cash lurks around every corner.

John 13:14–15 says, "Now that I, your Lord and Teacher, have washed your feet, you also should wash one another's feet. I have set you an example that you should do as I have done for you." Jesus set the example for us. He never asked anyone, "What's in it for Me?" And if we're following Him, neither will we.

I live with a servant and minister by the name of Amy Cunningham. Her days are spent asking us, "Can I get you anything?" She is such a wonderful example of our Savior. With guilt, she constantly asks herself, *Am I doing enough?* As a mom, daughter, pastor's wife, church employee, and friend, she often feels stretched. She feels as though she lets every person down who asks to spend time with her. She understands the concept of margin and declines invitations regularly in order to stay fresh and full.

I want my kids to serve their mom. I want them to hop off the couch and get their own drinks, cheese sticks, snacks, or sandwiches. What would our home look like if everyone, including me, constantly asked one another, "Can I get you anything?"

Keep in mind the spiritual journeys. Why in the world should I expect my children to serve around the house if they never observe me serving anyone myself? Our kids will pick up serving and loving from parents who model it on a regular basis.

Kids Who Brag about Jesus

Jesus said, "Whoever acknowledges me before men, I will also acknowledge him before my Father in heaven. But whoever disowns me before men, I will disown him before my Father in heaven" (Matt. 10:32–33).

I love surfing Facebook for the latest happenings in the families of Woodland Hills. You can learn a lot from their photos and posts. It shows how we value and raise our kids—though I admit that I have hidden a few friends for the excessive bragging they post online. Haley Toombs is not one of those parents.

Haley sings on our worship team. She and her husband, Hunter, are the parents of Haven. When school started back in August 2011, Haley posted the following lament and praise,

> I have been that guilty mom so many times as I put my sweet innocent child on the bus and off to public school, wondering if I'm doing the right thing as I plead the blood of Jesus over her to guard her heart and protect her. I know several of you have the same struggles, so please know my heart and allow me to share with no pride at all but pure humbleness that Haven led a child to Jesus on the bus today. This child comes from a broken home life and was sharing some of her sadness with Haven on their ride home. Haven shared with this child, in her seven-year-old version, how she really needs Jesus in her life to help her through her sadness, and the little girl agreed

and accepted Jesus Christ as her Lord and Savior. If I had given into that guilt or social pressure, Haven wouldn't have been riding that bus or going to a public school where she has been able to pray at lunch with children who don't even know who God is. I have peace that my/our children are right where God needs them to be and that He will take situations where our children could be robbed of their innocence and use them as his vessels to do His work and He will receive all the glory even in places where people have tried to shut Him out.[2]

Haley is taking a completely different angle on parenting. Is it my priority to raise happy, successful, Ivy League–educated, athletic superstars, or am I going to rejoice the day my child comes home and says, "I led a young person to Jesus today"? That puts it all in perspective for me.

Kids Who Love His Bride (the Church)

Do you love the church?

One pastor friend made a tragic mistake in raising his children. He intentionally set out to keep his ministry and his family separate. His heart was to protect his family and never bring his work home with him.

But today he lives with the regret that his grown children have no love for the church. They lack commitment to the local church and have little desire for connection to the body of Christ. My friend exceeded his original expectation, and now his children are detached completely from the church.

Spending several weeks a summer at family camps means a great deal of one-on-one time with families. In 2011, I made it my goal to personally ask this question of every parent: "Tell me about your church."

Here are a few of the answers I received.

"Well, we haven't been for a while, but I know we need to get back to it."

"Our church is okay, I just wish we had more (fill-in-the-blank)."

"We stopped going to the church we had been attending because the youth pastor (fill-in-the blank)."

"We've attended the same church forever but think it is time for a change."

Toward the end of our term at camp, after we developed some good relationships with families, we invited questions during my final teaching session. One dad asked, "Ted, I appreciate the idea of making Jesus the priority relationship in my child's life, but how do I do that practically?"

With a quivering lower lip, I replied, "I have asked almost each one of you this week to tell me about your church back home. To be honest with you I received lackluster answers from almost every person. No one was bubbling over with joy about his or her church. How can you expect your kids to love Jesus if you do not love His bride?"

I continued with, "If you want a relationship with Ted Cunningham, it kind of goes without saying that you also get a relationship with Amy Cunningham, my wife."

I joke with the Woodland Hills congregation that Branson is my home until I pastor each person at least once. Many people walk through our revolving door each year. I read the church-growth articles and make every effort to keep believers from exiting that door, but still they come, and sometimes they leave.

Let me ask you, what is the real issue? Is it the organization, leaders, church, or you? If you find fault in everything the church and the leaders do, more than likely your kids will watch you and repeat your choices. If you blast the pastor on the way home from church, your kids will repeat what they hear.

Teach your children Hebrews 13:17: "Obey your leaders and submit to their authority. They keep watch over you as men who must give an account. Obey them so that their work will be a joy, not a burden, for that would be of no advantage to you."

Trophy parenting destroys the church. Our temptation as leaders is to create programs and ministries to meet the demands and expectations of trophy parents, rather than confronting real heart issues. Avoid creating an attitude of entitlement in your children and instead impress on them a desire to serve. Your children's love for the bride of Jesus starts with your love for the bride of Jesus.

Lead, and they will follow.

Parent Gut Check

- Rate your relationship with Jesus. How connected are you? Very? Somewhat? Marginally?
- Do you know the words of Jesus? Are they your guide? Do you abide in His words?
- What are some ways you prioritize Jesus in your everyday life?

- Name a few people you served today. How did you serve them?
- Do you have any relationships that need to be reconciled? Who needs some love from you today?

Chapter 7
Preparing Our Children for the World

Letting go is hard.

Some parents delay allowing their children adulthood responsibilities as an antidote to failure, pain, risk, and potential loss. Keeping children at home means keeping them safe, while letting them venture out on their own means we are no longer in charge or control. That is scary.

In the airport last year I saw a mom from our church who was awaiting the arrival of her daughter and new granddaughter. She stood outside of security with a giddiness that was precious. I struck up a conversation.

"Who you waiting on?" I asked.

"My daughter is coming in with my one-year-old granddaughter. This is my first time meeting her," she replied.

"Congratulations," I said, then inquired, "Where are they flying in from?"

"New Zealand," she answered with a smirk.

"New Zealand?!" I restated as a question.

"Yeah, Ted, it is a good lesson for any parent who wants their child to travel and see the world before settling down. Your daughter could meet someone on that trip and settle down in New Zealand," she said, rolling her eyes.

Sending our children into the world is not enough. When we cut the strings, they need a place to land. Sending them out to explore, "sow their wild oats," avoid responsibility, or be successful is not the goal. We send them out in the name of Jesus, prepared for the real world.

Growing up, my dad's favorite line was, "Welcome to the real world!" He used it whenever he heard me use any of the following lines or excuses:

"It's not fair!"

"Twelve-year-olds shouldn't have to pay taxes."

"All the other kids get to!"

"I don't want to mow the lawn today."

"Can you believe my teacher gave us this much work to bring home?"

My dad's second favorite line was, "The world does not revolve around you, Teddy." Call it tough love if you want—he called it preparing love. Once you get into the real world, you realize how true that statement is.

Trophy parenting is overprotective. The overprotective parent lives under several lies and false presumptions about the way the world works. But we want our children to grow up learning the truth, not our false reality, about the way the world works.

Three Big Lies

Satan is the "prince of the power of the air" (Eph. 2:2 NASB). While God is ultimately in control, He allows Satan to operate on this earth, and according to Scripture Satan has domain over unbelievers, not believers. Followers of Jesus are no longer under the rule of Satan (Col. 1:13), while unbelievers are caught "in the snare of the devil" (2 Tim. 2:26 NASB).

Satan wants your children to adopt false beliefs about the world such as, "Look out for number one." "If it feels good, do it." "God is a liar." "I'm a good person." "I'm not that bad." "It's all about the money." "Take down whoever you need to to make it to the top."

Satan wants our children to serve themselves, deny God and His Word, and ultimately die separated from God. That is his plan.

This year, my kids and I studied the three big lies Satan gave Adam and Eve in the garden. These lies are in Genesis 3:4–5 and are more than applicable to us today.

"What are the three lies Satan fed us?" I ask the kids.

"You will not surely die. Your eyes will be opened. You will be like God," they repeat back to me.

"That's good. How do we still live by those lies today?" I continue to question.

Corynn responds, "We want to be our own God and do what we want, ignoring God."

Carson responds with, "We make up truth."

These are all great answers with practical applications for kids. While guarding our family from these lies, I worked with Carson on some things around the house. One morning before he left for school I asked him to work on three things: "Carson, I need you to start working on three things. One, shut off the lights when you leave a room. Two, flush the toilet. Three, stop throwing your clothes all over the floor after undressing. Got it?"

"Got it, Dad," he said as he headed out the door.

Toward the end of the week, I asked him, "Carson, what three things are we working on?"

"Dad, I promise, I got 'em," he said.

"I know, I know. I just want to hear them one more time," I insisted.

"Turn the lights off, flush the toilet, and I will not surely die," he said with a puzzled look on his face.

Even though one was a lie of Satan and the other two were things to work on around the house, he was so close that I accepted his answer. Preparing Carson for the world starts with an understanding of the Enemy and his lies. It then requires an awareness of evil.

The World Is Full of Evil

My mom taught me that evil exists and that I should be on the lookout for it—she bordered on paranoid, but in a good way. Years ago, parents sent their kindergartners to school free from the fear of predators. *Not anymore.*

Bonnie Cunningham had a special, discreet way of dealing with this kind of evil. When I hit the age where it was no longer appropriate for me to go into the women's bathroom, she sent me into the men's room alone with a grand announcement.

Picture an eight-year-old boy walking into the Fox Valley Mall food-court restroom with his mom holding open the door and shouting, "Teddy, if anyone touches you, scream bloody murder."

Subtle, Mom.

My mom has a booming voice, too, so the guys in the bathroom avoided me like the plague. She is a great mom.

On Sunday, September 11, 2011, I told my daughter about a day of great evil that also became a defining moment in our nation's history. On the tenth anniversary of 9/11, we watched twenty minutes of footage from those horrific events that have since shaped our nation.

We also planned a special remembrance at Woodland Hills Family Church that day to honor those who risk their lives for our safety and protection. As we drove to church I explained to Corynn and Carson the events of the day and why they would be seeing a Branson fire truck parked outside our church.

Earlier in the week, I asked our congregation through Facebook, "Where were you and what were you doing on September 11, 2001?" Here are some of the responses I shared with my kids and the congregation during the service that day.

> Jenna Jackson: I was pregnant and in Vegas; my two best friends got married that day. I had woken up early and gone down to the pool to not wake anyone else. They had the coverage playing over the loudspeaker. I went upstairs, knocking on everyone's doors, telling them to turn on the TV. Ending up being there an extra few days. The thing that sticks out in my mind the most is walking down the hotel's hallway over the next few days, and everyone's door was open.

Everyone wanted to feel closer to someone, even strangers.

Virginia Murphy: I was at home with my husband, watching in disbelief and horror. Spent most of the day in prayer.

Claudia Blakley Bolles: I was working at a Branson hotel front desk, hosting a WWII Reunion. Watching in disbelief and keeping the veterans calm as they were ready to go to war again.

Leah Melvin Steele: About to go on stage for a morning show.... They stopped the show, shared the news, had a moment of silence and prayer. Hardest show ever!

Bob Turas: At the time one of my largest accounts was the WTC Marriott. I was in shock trying to find out about friends there. I will never forget the loss and panic I felt that day.

Ted Martin: At fire station one ... watching live news coverage when the second plane hit the tower. I remember a reporter speaking about all of the fire alarms sounding.... The alarm sounds were personal safety system (PASS) devices worn by firefighters, activated due to [a] fall, laying still,

or expos[ure] to high heat. Those activated PASS
devices sent chills down our spines.[1]

The emotions of that day tell a story. In the car that Sunday
morning I shared some of these responses with my kids as we discussed the war, evil, and terrorism. My eight-year-old understood
clearly that lives were lost and how we processed the evil aggression
of that tragic day.

The problem of evil is a debate thousands of years old. If you
studied philosophy in college, you know the argument about evil
that "disproves" God's existence. It goes something like this: "One: if
an all-powerful, all-loving, and all-knowing God exists, then evil cannot. Two: there is evil in the world. Three: therefore an all-powerful,
all-loving, all-knowing, and perfectly good God cannot exist."

God exists; we know that. He is all-knowing (omniscient), all-
loving (omnibenevolent), and all-powerful (omnipotent). If there
exists an omnipotent, omniscient, and perfectly good God, how does
evil exist? Where does it come from? How do we deal with it?

Jesus gave us the answer: evil exists and flows from the heart:

> "Are you so dull?" he asked. "Don't you see that
> nothing that enters a man from the outside can
> make him 'unclean'? For it doesn't go into his
> heart but into his stomach, and then out of his
> body." (In saying this, Jesus declared all foods to
> be "clean.")
>
> He went on: "What comes out of a man is what
> makes him 'unclean.' For from within, out of men's

> hearts, come evil thoughts, sexual immorality …
> adultery, greed, malice, deceit, lewdness, envy, slan-
> der, arrogance and folly. All these evils come from
> inside and make a man 'unclean.'" (Mark 7:18–23)

Jesus was speaking to the source of evil, the heart of man. The events of 9/11 flowed from the hearts of evil men—not governments, a pagan deity, or a religious group.

One of the most important things we must teach our children is that people innately have evil in their hearts—and all parents attempt to protect or shelter their children from this evil. If a man broke into my house tonight to take my child's life, I have one option: I would protect him at all costs. Self-defense is justified, and taking the life of the assailant is acceptable.

I believe that one of the worst things parents can do is teach their children to look for the good in every person. It sounds sweet, loving, and the "Jesus way" of doing things, but it isn't shrewd. One of the greatest lies we teach our kids is that there is goodness inside all men, and you just have to look for it—but in reality, the opposite is true.

God is holy and perfect. We are sinful. Jesus is the mediator between God and man. As a pastor, the last thing I want is a person leaving a service on Sunday thinking, "I am not that bad of a person."

The apostle Paul taught that we are "objects of wrath" (Eph. 2:3) and "dead in transgressions" (v. 5) before Christ. Only Jesus brings us life.

We lost three thousand lives on 9/11. Our nation's guard was down. The 9/11 Commission Report stated it clearly:

We learned about an enemy who is sophisticated, patient, disciplined, and lethal.... It makes no distinction between military and civilian targets. *Collateral damage* is not in its lexicon.

We learned that the institutions charged with protecting our borders, civil aviation, and national security did not understand how grave this threat could be, and did not adjust their policies, plans, and practices to deter or defeat it....

We need to design a balanced strategy for the long haul, to attack terrorists and prevent their ranks from swelling while at the same time protecting our country against future attacks.[2]

The events of September 11, 2001, reshaped our nation, and we are better protected today because of heightened awareness. Travel through any airport and process your family through security to see firsthand the lasting effects of that day. Be prepared, not paranoid.

Ephesians 6:10–13 says,

Finally, be strong in the Lord and in his mighty power. Put on the full armor of God so that you can take your stand against the devil's schemes. For our struggle is not against flesh and blood, but against the rulers, against the authorities, against the powers of this dark world and against the spiritual forces of evil in the heavenly realms. Therefore put

on the full armor of God, so that when the day of
evil comes, you may be able to stand your ground,
and after you have done everything, to stand.

Satan is sophisticated and patient. He hates you and your child.
His purpose is simple: to keep you and your child from following
Jesus.

We must understand the gravity of this threat. I believe that it's
no accident that Ephesians 6:10–13 immediately follows the Bible's
central teaching on marriage and family in Ephesians 5:22–6:4. We
must design a balanced strategy for our families for the long haul,
which means putting on the full armor of God to prevent Satan from
future attacks. No weapon formed against us shall prosper.

Burying our head in the sand is not an option.

Isolationism

I grew up in an independent, fundamentalist, premillennial, King
James-version–only Baptist church. My family faithfully attended
every Sunday morning, Sunday night, and Wednesday night. The
church held a revival in the spring and one in the fall.

Our church was small and never broke the ceiling of two hundred people on a Sunday morning, and our pastor was a faithful man
who served that congregation for over thirty years. He was the leader,
and we did what we were told.

However, some of his fellow pastors were not quite as loving as
he was. I remember attending a revival my freshman year of college.
The guest speaker was a very angry fundamentalist preacher, and
this revival marked the first time I ever saw a man stand *on top* of

the pulpit. In my twenty years at this fundamentalist church, I saw pastors hit the pulpit and kick the pulpit, but this was the first time I'd ever seen a guy crawl up on top of the pulpit. I suppose his tactic worked, because it intimidated me.

Also, I'll never forget his words because they helped me transition out of the independent, fundamentalist Baptist church. His sermon covered what I call the Fundamentalist Five: Attendance, Hair, Movies, Bible Versions, and Women's Modesty.

He actually spoke these words: "I am sick and tired of you heffers struttin' around trying to stick fifty pounds of potatoes in a ten-pound sack." He was referring to larger women wearing tight-fitting jeans.

Was my church a cult? No. But they certainly had cultlike tendencies. I sometimes hear on the news of a church that builds walls, creates a compound for its members, and starts buying guns; the people of that church are isolating themselves from the world. Cutting themselves off from the world is one step ahead of drinking Kool-Aid.

Parents, take heed; this is not what Jesus taught. One of the most gripping and emotional prayers of the Bible is found in John 17. Jesus was about to hang naked on a cross before His creation and take all the past and future sins of the world on Himself. Before He went to the cross He prayed to His Father in heaven. He prayed for Himself, His disciples, and me (a future follower).

In that moment, Jesus prayed to His Daddy these words:

> My prayer is not that you take them out of the
> world but that you protect them from the evil

one. They are not of the world, even as I am not
of it. Sanctify them by the truth; your word is
truth. As you sent me into the world, I have sent
them into the world. For them I sanctify myself,
that they too may be truly sanctified. (John
17:15–19)

My murdered Savior did not pray for isolation for His children
from the world; rather, He asked that the Father protect them from
the Evil One.

Our devotional time as a family that Sunday of 9/11/11 was the
W from our family devotional cards. Jesus said, "Go! I am sending
you out like lambs among wolves" in Luke 10:3. Jesus is our Good
Shepherd, and we are His sheep. Why then does Jesus send us out
to the world?

The apostle Paul gave this warning to believers as they interact with
the world: "Do not conform any longer to the pattern of this world,
but be transformed by the renewing of your mind" (Rom. 12:2).

Some parents hover and shelter their kids to keep them from
this world of evil. Unfortunately, this strategy is not an option for
the long haul. Preparing our children for the world means that we
understand they must leave our care one day and live on their own.
Effective parenting moves them in that direction and gives them the
tools necessary to be in the world, but not of it.

Carson and the Kindergarten Playground

I recently cohosted a radio show with Susie Larson out of Minnesota.
Susie has such an incredible heart for her listeners, and she regularly

turns her talk show into a prayer and praise show to encourage and minister to her audience.

On the day I was on the show, one mom called in for prayer and was quite distraught. She had sent her firstborn, a four-year-old, off to preschool earlier that day. I hope my chuckle went unheard. Before we prayed, I said, "You think preschool is tough, but wait until kindergarten." In other words, "Mom, this is just the beginning of your job as a parent. This child will not be with you forever, and the sooner you embrace that, the sooner little Johnnie launches."

When Carson started kindergarten we prepared him for dealing with difficult people, teaching him how not to be a difficult person: "Take turns." "Listen to your teacher." "Walk in line in the hallways." "Raise your hand before you talk." "Get along with others on the playground."

On day one, Carson made a new friend, and they formed a club called the Bulldogs. It was an open club, and they welcomed everyone. They spent both recesses each day running sprints. Fast or slow, they accepted you into the club.

By the end of the week, Carson's new friend asked him to leave the club. When Carson jumped in the car after school, he broke into tears. Explaining the story to his mom, he worked through the rejection by saying, "My friend is the most conceited person I know. He only thinks of himself."

The time at dinner that night was sweet. These teaching opportunities are defining moments. They are a great opportunity to listen, understand, and validate feelings.

"Carson, I heard you had a bad day," I said.

"I have good news and bad news," he responded.

"Give me the good news," I said.

"I got a smiley face today," he said with his own smile. This smiley-face sticker is the mark a student receives at his school for good behavior. Students receive them daily.

"What's the bad news?" I asked.

"My friend kicked me out of the Bulldogs. He didn't even have a good reason but said I couldn't be his friend anymore," he said, choking back tears. At that moment, every parent wants to come to the rescue.

I wanted to say, "Your friend is a jerk, and you deserve better. Walk away. Don't worry about him. Make new friends."

Against my own emotions, I went in a different direction.

I told him, "Carson, do you know what Jesus said? He said, 'Love your enemies and pray for those who persecute you.' We are to love our enemies, and Jesus said so. We can't hate."

While teaching our children to walk away protects them and their emotions in the short run, Jesus had a different approach: love and pray. Simple enough.

That night before bed, we all took turns praying. I started and prayed for protection from the Evil One and thanked God for the many blessings in our home. Amy and Corynn prayed after me. Batting cleanup was Carson, and his short prayer caught us off guard.

"God, I pray that my friend will not have nightmares tonight and that he will have a good morning tomorrow. In Jesus's name, amen," Carson said.

Enough said!

Sending our children off to kindergarten and junior high and high school foreshadows what we can expect when we send them off to college. I regularly visit college campuses and have the opportunity for some good conversations with campus pastors and professors. One recurring message I receive is their concern for the freshmen's inability to cope, make decisions, or function without their parents' involvement.

Prayer from Evil

Samuel Rodriguez is a speaker for Men at the Cross and a leader for the National Hispanic Evangelical Association. From the time he was a small child, his dad prayed this prayer over him: "Father, cover Sammy in the blood of Jesus, protect him from evil, and fulfill Your purpose in his life."

When Samuel shared that story with me, I immediately implemented that prayer in the Cunningham home. I never leave home or allow my kids out of the car without praying a version of that prayer over them.

Friday morning is one of the most spiritual days of my week. I feel close to the Lord as I wheel our garbage cans down the driveway and place them on the curve. As I make the turn to head back to the garage, I walk slowly while I look at our house.

I pray these words: "Father, cover this home in the blood of Jesus. Protect us from evil. Fulfill Your purpose in our lives."

Amy and I observe parents at our church to gain deeper insight into our own parenting style. We look for close-knit families who serve Jesus, admit their mistakes, and recover with grace. Rob and Susan Robbins are parents we love to watch.

They are not helicopter parents, hovering all the time, but they had every reason to be. Rob walked away from corporate America for his family, and he allowed his kids to fail in painful, heart-wrenching ways. They raised four great kids who love Jesus and are well-prepared for the world.

Their daughter, Shantell, is kicking Satan's hind-end all over the place. She is a twenty-three-year-old single young woman who serves kids in the inner city of Memphis. She lives on a meager salary and is content in her service. Our church recently helped Shantell take a trip to Africa to rescue young women from the sex-trade industry. Rob and I had dinner with Shantell while traveling through Memphis the other night, and she shared story after story about how the Holy Spirit is directing her all over the country and world.

I asked Rob after dinner, "How do you and Susan handle the many adventures of Shantell Robbins?"

Rob said, "Prayer." He knows Shantell is traveling to some dangerous places around the world, but he sends her knowing she is covered in the blood of Jesus.

Their oldest son, Shay, is a director at Kanakuk Kamps and spends his summers working with teens under the leadership of Joe White. He is quite the preacher, teacher, husband, and father. But before this, Shay spent many years living the lies of Satan in Southern California.

How did his life turn around? *His parents prayed.*

Their youngest son, Blake, recently got married. He is twenty-one and a mixed martial artist and husband to his wife, Chloe. How are Mom and Dad dealing with losing their last born from the home? Prayer, especially right before Blake heads into the ring for an MMA fight.

Rob and Susan's middle son, Nick, walked into a retail store at age sixteen and committed armed robbery. Convicted of the crime, he served seven and a half years in prison. He gave his life to Jesus while in prison. He is now a member and leader at Woodland Hills and works full-time in prison ministry.

What got Nick through? *Prayer.*

Parent Gut Check

- What are some ways we shelter and isolate our children from the world?
- Where is the line between protecting and preparing our children?
- What is your view of the world?
- What are you doing to prepare your children for the evil hearts of others?
- Are you praying with your children? What is your prayer?

Chapter 8
Adulthood Milestones

Life is full of transitions. From birth on, we enter one state of transition after another. Hospital to home. Breast to bottle. Crib to bed. Diapers to toilet. Fits of emotions to words. Home to school. Kindergarten to first grade. Elementary to junior high then to high school. High school to college. In some cases, people go to community college, then on to college. College to career. Independence to marriage. Honeymoon to baby. Baby to multiple kids. Kids to empty nest. Empty nest to retirement. Retirement to nursing home. Then on to Jesus.

Have you ever thought about what life would look like for our kids if one of those transitions simply didn't happen? What would it look like if our kids never left the crib or high chair?

Our doctor has delivered thousands of babies over the course of his career. He has a very relaxed style, especially about early childhood development. He answered most of our fretting questions about our baby with, "If it continues into kindergarten, then we will start worrying." Great answer. It relaxed me, but not Amy.

Some parents plan for each transition, and all of us love some transitions more than others. Some transitions save us money, like the end of diapers. Some transitions cost us money, like our kids going to college. Some make us cry, while others create a sense of loss. But without these transitions, we stop learning and growing.

Taking Off the Training Wheels

Carson learned how to ride his bike the summer he turned six. We live in the Ozarks, where flat roads are hard to find, but Dogwood Canyon is a six-mile bike trail in southwest Missouri that has plenty of shade for hot days and grass on each side for those early spills.

At the risk of using a cliché, learning to ride a bike is a strong metaphor for the transitions into adulthood.

Like most kids, Carson loved his training wheels. They were comfortable. Coasting down a hill with his training wheels on, his hands in the air, gave him a sense of safety and security. The thought of removing them struck fear in him. I remember sharing the news with him and receiving the "Dad, why would you do this to me?" look.

As kindergarten drew near, Amy and I felt it was time to take them off. I had no idea how many emotions he was about to experience. He begged and begged us to let him ride his scooter through the canyon instead.

I took the training wheels off before we loaded up the family's bikes in the car and drove out to the canyon.

On the way there, Carson asked, "How long are we riding our bikes today?"

"Let's wait and see, Carson. We are going to take our time and enjoy the ride," I responded.

Like most parents, we spent more time explaining the joys of bike riding than explaining that it required hard work.

"Carson, kindergartners ride on two wheels, not four," I said.

When we arrived at Dogwood Canyon, Carson asked, "Would it be okay if I just run beside you guys?" This was a battle of wills.

I left the kickstand on my bike down and reached for his red and blue Transformers bike. He hopped on reluctantly. Carson learning to ride his bike was for the good of the whole family.

Momentum is the first skill necessary for riding a bike without training wheels. Balance and braking come only after you learn that speed is your friend. Balancing is easier when you are moving.

Amy and I took turns running alongside Carson for the first mile. He fought at first, but his fighting faded as we went further along the canyon.

I'll always remember Amy, Corynn, and me shouting for his first hundred-yard solo ride.

"Carson, you are doing it! We knew you could!" we all shouted. He smiled.

The next lesson was braking. Initially when Carson wanted a pit stop, he found a soft piece of ground or a shrub and dumped the bike. He hopped off and let the bike do its own thing.

"Since Mom and I don't jump out of the car when we want it to stop, you can tap on your brake like we do," I told him.

Learning to ride a bike is all about perspective. We, who learned how to ride many years ago, forget how hard it was to remember everything at once. I liken it to golf. One of the reasons I stink at golf is because I have a hard time keeping all the steps in my head.

You know the biking lesson is complete when your child starts and stops on his own. Of course, Carson now knows how to position his left pedal and give himself three pushes to get started. He stops with a touch of the brakes. He knows how to gain speed going up a hill and coast going down.

We went back to Dogwood Canyon a few weeks after we took off the training wheels, and the whole family pedaled about two miles out. When we told Carson to head back to the car, he wanted to stay and keep riding.

Once we overcome the fear of learning something new, it becomes as simple as riding a bike. With our kids, we resist the milestones of adulthood because of fear.

Our children have milestones that measure their growth. Age is the most obvious milestone, and we celebrate that milestone with a birthday party. Age determines much in our culture as we place children in age-graded sporting activities, schools, and Sunday school classes. We measure their learning by grade level.

Invented in 1904, the term *adolescence* stems from the Latin *adolescere*, which means "to grow up."[1] This man-made age is when a person is no longer a child but not yet an adult. I call it limbo. Others call adolescence a vacation from responsibility.

Scripturally and historically, there are two life phases in the development of a young man: *childhood* and *adulthood*. The apostle Paul explained this transition in 1 Corinthians, where he wrote, "When I was a child, I talked like a child, I thought like a child,

I reasoned like a child. When I became a man, I put childish ways behind me" (13:11).

Growing from a child to an adult meant leaving home, finishing education, securing employment, marrying, and starting a family. All five of these milestones happened quickly, if not simultaneously. Nowhere in Scripture is there a wide gap between childhood and adulthood. But today we have such a gap.

It is called adolescence.

My wife's grandparents have a fascinating story of the milestones. Lloyd returned from World War II and went to work at Hormel Foods in Austin, Minnesota. He met Lorraine soon after, and they went on their first date on a Saturday. The following Saturday Lloyd asked Lorraine, "Are we going to get serious about this relationship or what?"

"What do you mean?" she asked him.

"Do you want to get married?" he said, and just like that he popped the question.

She said, "Yes." They married the next Saturday.

So, follow this sequence of events: they had their first date on a Saturday, got engaged the following Saturday, and married one another on the third Saturday. In September of 2011, Lloyd and Lorraine celebrated sixty-five years of marriage. We define their generation by the principles of duty, loyalty, honor, commitment, and sacrifice.

But today, adolescence starts in the early teen years and for some continues on into the thirties. Young people today struggle with the when and how of growing up. Trophy parents, churches, schools, and our culture in general place little to no pressure on them to become adults.

This week I had the opportunity to teach at the Kanakuk Linkyear, a gap-year program between high school and college. I told Adam Donyes, the program's director, to count me in so long as the program was not a delay of adulthood. He assured me it was not. Adam is a thirty-one-year-old go-getter for Jesus. He has passion and drive that the Linkyear students see and understand.

My topic for the Linkyear students was milestones of adulthood and relationships. We discussed entitlement for an entire morning. I planned on fifteen or so minutes, but we spent hours discussing the students' desire to leave home, grow up, and take on responsibility. It refreshed me until I heard that Mom and Dad were the roadblocks. Here's the feedback I heard from several of them:

"I want to get a job and work my way through college, but my parents won't let me."

"My parents think a job is too much pressure while attending school, and they want me to wait until after college to work."

"What do I need to do to prove to my parents that I am ready to be on my own and that I do not need them hovering over me?"

I appreciated their words because they flowed from hearts that understand entitlement. Most of these students came from homes and families of great wealth and privilege. When I asked, "How many of you would consider yourself entitled?" over three-quarters of the room raised their hands. The fact that they identify this in their hearts means over half the battle is already won.

While I taught that day, Adam received many phone calls. He quietly dismissed himself outside the room, and I saw him through the window, talking at length to several callers. Any guess who the callers were? Parents! It was Mom and Dad checking up on their kids to make sure everything was good.

I say, cut those strings, Mom and Dad.

Prolonged adolescence as it exists now is an extended vacation from responsibility. Becoming an adult means leaving home, making wise adult decisions, and taking responsibility for the outcome of those decisions. Parents wait too long to teach their kids to be adults, and intentionally or unintentionally, they prolong their children's journey into adulthood.

Is there something wrong with being handed privilege? No. The key is to link the privilege with responsibility. Vacation comes *after* a season of work. The reward comes on the back end, not the front end.

I've yet to meet a parent who says, "I do not want to raise responsible adults." But instead of favoring responsibility, we start with privilege at a very early age and continuously delay responsibility.

You can ask my kids, "What is Daddy's definition of maturity?"

Their answer is, "I will not be with Mom and Dad forever, so plan accordingly."

Amen.

Milestone #1: Leave Home

Leaving means to forsake, depart from, leave behind, and abandon. From the moment your child is born, you are entrusted to raise that child with the goal of preparing him or her to ultimately leave your home. It's a hard truth to swallow when you swaddle a baby who is entirely dependent on your constant oversight and support. The work that goes into the early years of child rearing forms a tight bond.

There are three key reasons for embracing a "leave and cleave" parenting style.

First, this parenting style starts children on their spiritual journey and prepares them for adulthood. Adulthood defined is taking personal responsibility for your thoughts, emotions, actions, and reactions. Teaching your children that they will not be with you forever and to plan accordingly begins them on the journey toward becoming adults. Instead of teaching our kids to remain dependent on us always, we teach them to live independent of us.

Second, the "leave and cleave" parenting style guards parents from becoming too overprotective. Hovering parents communicate through word and deed that their children cannot be trusted. Understanding the parenting implications of the "leave and cleave" texts continually reminds us that our children need to take chances, make mistakes, learn, and go on. As parents we become monitors of their progress rather than controllers of their behavior.

Later in life, the difficulties continue when hovering parents control and manipulate their adult children after they marry. This is often an attempt to get their needs for love met. Understanding the "leave and cleave" parenting style guards against becoming an overprotective, dominant, and controlling parent.

Third, the "leave and cleave" parenting style establishes order in the home. This parenting style constantly reminds kids that they are a welcome addition to the family and that they won't be here forever. It reminds them that Mom and Dad will remain together and enjoy life long after they are gone. How many times do you see families where the kids operate with an attitude that says, "What in the world will Mom and Dad do with their time once I'm gone?" After all, the school years these days are all about Mom and Dad attending games, carpooling, and paying for their kids' cell phones. What will the parents' purpose in life be during the empty-nesting years? Of course, I ask that question rhetorically, with my tongue firmly lodged in my cheek.

Separation from parents is good and healthy. Good parents recognize the blessing that every child needs to one day be released to a new journey with Christ and his or her mate. Our children need the confidence that they will one day make capable, adult decisions on their own.

I talk to adult children all the time who call home in their twenties and thirties, asking their parents for money. Then they get angry over how their parents are so controlling. Hello! I first tell them to get their *Star Wars* sheets off the bed. Then I tell them firmly that they must grow up.

During premarital counseling, I make sure young couples get this. The conversation usually goes something like this: "Before you call home asking for money, think through the interest payments. You have no idea how much it will cost you to borrow two hundred dollars. You will pay on it for years. You will pay with the interest of lack of trust, controlling maneuvers, and occasional guilt trips."

Age does not determine adulthood. Eighteen is the legal age of an adult in this country, but I know very few eighteen-year-old adults. Adulthood defined means making adult decisions on your own. It's about taking personal responsibility for your actions, words, reactions, and decisions. It's about making right decisions even when you're not being watched.

Milestone #2: Finish School

I grew up in a non-sports family. We played sports, we watched sports, but compared to some of the college fans I know, we were bandwagon fans (which is a derogatory term used by true sports fans).

Kanakuk Family Kamp in Branson hosts a college night each term. After dinner on the selected night they play through several college fight songs, and honestly, they all sound the same to me. Last year on college night, we shared our table with a family from Oklahoma University and another family from Oklahoma State University. One school's colors are red and the other orange. These people were very passionate alumni!

At the end of the fight-song playlist, a group of twenty or so counselors gathered in the corner and started chanting, "Small Christian school, small Christian school, small Christian school!" That was the highlight for me.

Our obsession for achievement leads us to push college down the throats of every child, but the truth is that college is not for everyone. We need trade workers, retail-store clerks, waiters, and waitresses. For some, combining this milestone with the third milestone is called an apprenticeship, which is a very wise choice for learning a trade.

Parents treat college as a last-ditch effort to secure their child's future. It is now assumed that every high school graduate will head off to college when the fact is some young people spend a year or two in college and decide that it's not for them. That's okay. Men and women alike can choose occupations that do not require college degrees.

I attended Oswego High School in Oswego, Illinois, which was a progressive school in the trades. My freshman year I spent six weeks each in metal shop, woodshop, graphic arts, automotive class, home economics, drafting, and agriculture. Graphic arts was the only class I warmed up to. My brother, on the other hand, took to woodshop very well under the mentoring of his teacher Mr. Groth.

My brother spent his junior and senior years leaving school for half a day for building trades class, which involved building an entire house from the ground up over the course of the school year. My brother loved it and made it his career. This milestone may or may not include a four-year degree. Apprenticeships, trade schools, and on-the-job vocational training suit other needs in the workplace.

I married Amy in 1996, right between her junior and senior years at Liberty University. We thought about delaying our marriage a year to let her finish her senior year on campus, but that was too long for both of us to wait. Instead, we benefitted from the blessing of Liberty's extended-learning program. Amy finished her degree through correspondence.

I remember the day I asked Amy's dad for her hand in marriage.

"Mr. Freitag, I would like to marry your daughter. May I please have your blessing?" I asked.

"You betcha," he said in his thick Norwegian accent.

"One more thing. I would like to pay for Amy's last year of school," I said.

That got me a double, "You betcha!"

I wanted to accomplish the first milestones in a few short years. Delaying work and marriage for college was unnecessary in our situation. Our parents supported our decision because they saw our drive for getting established and launching into ministry.

Milestone #3: Start Work

Twenty hours a week is not full-time! Wow, I had to get that off my chest.

Parents, I beg you, please teach that simple rule to your kids—as any potential employer of your child will tell you, they need to bring a strong work ethic to the job market.

My friend Larry was twenty-five years old and clueless about life in the real world. I truly love and care for the guy, but when it came to work he was apathetic and carried an attitude of entitlement. He called me one day and asked if I would meet him for lunch. He had lost his job and was mad. So we met.

"I don't know what's going on, Ted. I've had five jobs in a year, and none of them worked out," he said.

"Let's start at the beginning. Tell me about the first job and why it did not work out," I said.

"My boss was relentless, asking me to be there at eight every morning," he said with a look of surprise. After he voiced his frustration over boss number two not letting him have his birthday off, I stopped him and shared with him the common denominator principle: "Larry, wherever you go, there you are. What is the one thing true about your past five jobs?" I asked.

"What do you mean?" he asked.

"You are the common denominator, Larry!" I said. "It is not about finding you the right job, whatever that means. It is about you growing up and taking personal responsibility for your life and work."

He started to get it.

One book that helped me understand the Millennial Generation was *The Trophy Kids Grow Up: How the Millennial Generation Is Shaking Up the Workplace* by Ron Alsop.

Ron praises the Millennial Generation by clearly defining their strengths:

- Great concern for those around them
- Team-oriented, they love meetings and spending time together
- Technologically savvy
- Global thinkers
- Great compassion
- Efficient and effective when given clear directions
- Appreciate diversity[2]

What a great assessment. I observe these traits firsthand in the millennials that attend Woodland Hills Family Church. In particular, I've seen that the millennials are leading the church back to helping the poor and caring for the widows and orphans and foreign missions.

When David Platt's book *Radical* came out, the millennials at our church devoured it. Before I even had time to read it, the twenty-somethings had developed a disdain for "stuff." David's book is all about taking back your faith from the American dream, a theme with which I agree.

My primary concern was with the way the book was applied by many young folks in our church. Less stuff meant less work, but stuff is not necessarily bad. God enables us to enjoy stuff (1 Tim. 4:4–5), and so long as we receive it with gratefulness and thanksgiving we can enjoy what we have. Also, I wanted the young people to know that hard work earns money and stuff that we can then give to the poor, the widows, the orphans, and foreign missions.

I hope you encourage your children to begin working before they leave home. This milestone is critical because it determines everything about the economics of your final two milestones: providing for your spouse and children.

Encourage them to work hard. You can't do anything with money if you don't have any. "Go to the ant, you sluggard; consider its ways and be wise!" (Prov. 6:6). The type of work your kids do is a part of whatever competency they develop, but hard work is a character issue.

Hard work also means that they're willing to do any job while they wait for the "perfect" job to come along. Don't let them grow up to be like Cousin Eddie from the movie *Christmas Vacation*, who refused to work because he was holding out for a management position. Cousin Eddie is a little boy. Do anything until you find the perfect fit.

Encourage the millennials to give generously. The first thing we do after we get our paychecks is give some away. After that, we put some money away and save it!

The last thing we do is spend. To become a reliable man or woman of God you must learn to produce more than you consume.

Milestone #4: Get Married

Whether your child is a five-year-old or a fifteen-year-old, I implore you to begin celebrating and promoting marriage in your home. This is an often-neglected milestone in our culture of prolonged adolescence.

Trophy parenting and the kid-centered home dishonor marriage in two ways. They indirectly erode Mom and Dad's marriage, and they do not equip children for their future marriage.

Child psychologist Vivian Friedman noted that changes in marriage magnify this trophy child culture: "There's been a whittling away of the bond between husband and wife, and an intensifying of the relationship between the parent and the child."[3]

Hebrews 13:4 has become a life verse for my family's ministry. It says, "Marriage should be honored by all, and the marriage bed kept pure." Esteeming marriage as highly valuable is our battle cry. Marriage is to be lifted up by every man, woman, senior, and child. My family travels with me around the country each month as I encourage couples and churches to honor marriage. Most churches and pastors I know are pro-marriage, pro-love, and some are even pro-dating.

Many pastors regularly teach on marriage in the church, but not all. Many churches have solid ministries or counselors in place for couples in crisis, but not all. Some churches and pastors consider their annual couples conference or marriage retreat the extent of their marriage emphasis. But honoring marriage should include the following:

- Teaching marriage as normative and singleness as the exception

- Encouraging the marrying of widows and adopting their children as your own
- Teaching young people to honor marriage, not just purity
- Offering marriage classes that prepare young adults for marriage
- Eradicating the kid-centered home
- Eliminating prolonged adolescence

By eradicating the kid-centered home we prioritize the spiritual journey and the model of the gospel of Jesus. The first part of Genesis 2:24 offers the "leave" teaching and begins our children on a path toward marriage. The "cleave" part recognizes that marriage happens early in the journey into adulthood. There is absolutely no need for a gap between the leave and cleave.

However, the social pressures of today say, "Learn to be independent first, so you can have a better marriage later." Independence has become a socially acceptable term for selfishness. Our children grow comfortable with the world revolving around them, and another ten years of that sounds good.

When a crisis couple walks into my office I always picture them as wearing two opposing sports jerseys. Since I am a Chicago Cubs fan, I picture one wearing the jersey of the Cubs and the other wearing the jersey of the St. Louis Cardinals. This visual helps me because usually at this point, they are not on the same team. My goal is that they replace their existing jerseys with a brand-new team jersey. My prayer is for them to be teammates rather than opponents.

My observation after counseling hundreds of couples is that the kid-centered home is destroying the future marriages of our children. A childhood spent receiving excessive praise and privilege does not translate into a marriage in which you deny yourself and serve the desires of your spouse.

The older my children get, the more they understand the importance of Mommy and Daddy loving and enjoying each other. On his third week of kindergarten, Carson said out of the blue, "If you and Mom ever got a divorce, school would become my favorite place to be."

While we think a home centered on the children shows love, there is one thing that shows more love, security, and safety: a mom and dad enjoying each other for life.

Picture a special future for your children's marriage. When they express their emotions of love, desire, or passion, hold them by the hand and walk a little bit. Don't shut them down. I learned this principle from Dr. Kevin Leman.

When your kid comes home and says, "I want a pony," play with the idea for a little bit. Don't immediately launch into, "We can't afford a pony. Where is the pony going to live? Who is going to feed the pony? You? Yeah, maybe for a week, but then you'll get bored and leave it up to me."

Good questions, bad approach.

A better approach would be, "Wouldn't it be fun to own a pony? I could see you riding the pony to school or the store when I need you to get me something. Next time we are at the zoo, let's stop by the ponies and see which color you like."

You can do the same thing with love and marriage.

My daughter, Corynn, is eight years old. One day, years from now, Corynn will come home and tell me she has met the man she will marry. At that moment, my plan is to pause, take a deep breath, and praise my Father in heaven for what He molds and forms in my children.

When Corynn started kindergarten, the best part of my day was dropping her off at school each morning at 8:30 a.m. The second best part of my day was picking her up from school in the afternoon. I'll never forget the day she told me about a little boy whom we'll call "Jason."

"He likes me, Dad," she said.

"Really?!" I asked.

"Yep, and I think I like him," she said with one eye closed and head slightly tilted, waiting for my response.

I'd prepared for this day, and I wanted to encourage her. No overreacting. Too many parents freak out at the signs of young love, and I was not going to be one of them. I would avoid statements like "You're too young!" "What?! You don't need to have a boyfriend at this age!" "You can't like him!" or "Boys are evil!"

Do you hear the "We can't afford a pony" tone in those answers?

What we think and want to say is, "I wish you didn't have these feelings at such an early age," "Stop feeling that way," or "You'll get over it, and I hope pretty quick!" Fight every urge to shut down your child's feelings. Rebuke anti-marriage feelings in the name of Jesus.

Corynn was not prepared for my response.

"Well, honey, do you think he is *the one*?" I asked her.

"DAD!" was all she could say.

I was prepared to go further. Inspired by Dr. Greg Smalley, I was ready to help her work on her first family budget and look for their first place. Greg allowed his elementary-school–aged daughter to go so far as to plan where she and her boyfriend would live after they wed, how they would make a living, and even set the date of the wedding. Once they crunched the numbers together, she saw that it did not seem feasible.

Milestone #5: Start a Family

The first four milestones prepare you for and feed into this final milestone. You leave your family, create healthy boundaries, and start your own. School prepares you to make a living, and it may also be the place where you find a spouse. You work to provide for others, not simply to consume for yourself. Finally, marriage joins you to another to make babies, raise them, and start this cycle again. Solomon spoke of this cycle when he said, "Generations come and generations go, but the earth remains forever" (Eccl. 1:4).

In my last book, *Young and in Love: Challenging the Unnecessary Delay of Marriage*, I found myself becoming judgmental of young people who unnecessarily delayed marriage. The Lord really worked on me in the process of writing that book. Before I judge the toothpicks in my neighbor's eye, I need to take a look at the gargantuan log sticking out of my face (my paraphrase of Matthew 7).

Amy and I waited seven years before starting our family. We delayed children for the exact reasons many young adults today delay marriage. Achieving independence, finding financial security, establishing careers, and finishing school were at the top of our list of reasons to delay having kids.

"I don't plan on anything changing," I declared to our small group after Amy and I received these words from our doctor: "Congratulations, you are expecting!"

I was full of excitement but long on ignorance. It doesn't help to make stupid statements like that when you are in a small group with three marriage and family therapists. "What do you mean nothing will change?" the group asked me collectively.

"The church is young and growing, and we will keep right on track," I assured everyone (as their pastor).

The snickering began. Three of the five couples had multiple children, and my ignorance was obvious to them. So they shared a dose of reality with me.

"Ted, I see this in a lot of couples," one member of the group shared. "They get married, and one or both parents want to maintain aspects of single life. They continue to regularly have boys' nights out multiple times a week, attend games and practices with their team, and go to the gym for workouts alone. Then they have kids. I know of one mom who still goes out clubbing several nights a week, leaving her two-year-old at home,"

"Yeah, I'm not doing any of that. Heck, I never did that when I was single," I self-righteously declared.

He continued, "Okay, for you it is meetings, visits, and studying, but it is the same idea. You will need to learn to say no to people like you haven't in the past."

I armed myself and was ready for a fight because serving the church was our life. Long nights preparing for holiday performances or vacation Bible school were routine for us. Dinners out with members of the church were normal, staff outings became a way of life, and we loved every minute of it.

Our small group formed around the same time we started Woodland Hills Family Church. Getting a church off the ground required a ton of time and two tons of energy. Our workweeks averaged sixty-plus hours, but we never complained about it because it was our passion. The work overflowed into our lives, and it consumed our conversations, trips to the store, and evening laptop time. There was always something to do. Since Amy and I were the only two staff members of a five-hundred-member church, it was on us to "git 'r' done." My plan was to buy a BabyBjörn, strap the child in, and away we go. From clueless to brainless!

"Nothing is going to change once the baby is born," I declared with the same authority as the president delivering the State of the Union address.

While I defended my pastorate to our small group, I had no idea what my words did to my wife. She sat there in silence. Who would have thought she was on the side of the other small-group participants? I meant no harm by my words; they were simply my attempt to assure everyone that the church was in good hands. But I had no idea how badly what I said hurt Amy. The fallout from those ill-chosen words changed our marriage. More importantly, it changed me.

Amy heard my words different from the way I meant them, and they rocked her world. She heard, "We are still going to work long hours each week. We will still go out to dinner regularly with friends. We will continue to put in long nights at church. Don't expect our lives or schedules to be any different." Nothing could have been further from the reality that would soon engulf our lives. Balancing marriage, career, and parenting would prove to be the greatest challenge of my life.

Later that night, Amy shared with me, "Ted, I hope you know things are going to change. The baby will need naps, regular feedings, and a schedule." Her beautiful eyes grabbed my attention, and I could feel her heart as she gently said, "Everything is going to change." Little did I know, she was exactly right.

Parenting, like marriage, keeps you from selfishness. We need more men and women to embrace this fifth milestone with great tenacity and determination. We must balance work, prioritize marriage, and raise our kids to do the same.

Preparing Our Kids for Marriage and Sex

At every marriage seminar I teach, I reserve the final session for a candid conversation about sex. When the session ends, I always hear these questions: "How do we talk to our kids about sex? Where do we start? How far do we go?" Parents know this is a major part of growing up and preparing our children for life and marriage. I want to encourage you to start talking about sex early and remain clear, candid, open to questions, and don't ever stop.

I grew up in a church and home that featured minimal discussion of sex. In an attempt to protect their children's virginity and "innocence," some parents fall into the trap of employing some kind of shame-based sex education. They use code words and minimal details, and every conversation is cloaked in shyness when addressing the issue of sex. This sort of education often results in the children believing that sex is unmentionable or even dirty. It often creates a guilt-prone sex life later on.

I am sick and tired of Christian parents feeling they need to enter Satan's turf when discussing sex—this is not his turf! Sex is on God's turf! God is holy, and He created sex for married partners to enjoy. As a pastor, I am concerned about the sex life of each family member at our church. I want each church member to have great sex in God's context, and I want each child to know that God created sex and it's fantastic!

Start reading. Discover truths about sex, sexuality, and sexual intimacy straight from Scripture. Exhaust God's Word to gain an understanding of what He created in sex.

Start talking. The "sex talk" commonly known as the "birds and the bees" is dead. Good riddance! With the Internet, social media, and mobile devices, we need to begin a long conversation with our kids that starts in preschool and continues through to marriage. Our children are exposed to innuendo and images at a far earlier age, so we need to start early.

Stop the silence. We must reclaim sex as a topic that is addressed first by churches and parents, not Hollywood, the music industry, or the schools. Be the first to write messages of sex and sexuality on your child's heart and beat the world to the punch.

Birth to Five Years Old

The best way to approach kids with the subject of sex is with prayer, grace, love, and honesty. All too often parents fall into the unhealthy pattern of using code words, a practice usually started when kids are young.

When Corynn was four, she asked a lot of questions, and some of them dealt with sexuality. She asked, "What is that on Carson?" Rather than use terms like "pee-pee" or "tally-wacker," I told her, "That's your brother's penis."

It's important to understand and communicate what's appropriate and what's not. But when we start using code names and trying to hide the truth behind the birds and the bees and all of that, we rob our children of knowing the truth and becoming comfortable with who they are and who God created them to be.

While Corynn and I were on a walk one day we saw an older girl approaching us. She piped up and said, "She's a girl too, right, Daddy?"

"Yeah, she's a girl," I confirmed.

"She has breasts. I don't have those," she said.

"Well, one day I will buy you a training bra!" I responded. "Won't that be exciting on the day your breasts start forming? That will happen in about eight or so years."

Back then my daughter didn't know the difference between ten years and ten minutes, so she regularly checked to see if she was there yet.

During preschool, a child's brain develops rapidly. If you teach such young children that their bodies are shameful things, and you do that in the most subtle ways, then they'll believe it for years to come. That's why it's so important to avoid code names and to be honest with your children.

Six to Nine Years Old
Teach them about modesty, sexuality, and the difference between appropriate and inappropriate touching.

Once, when Carson was at my parents' house a well-endowed woman came on the news. He told my parents that she was "showing her line." Of course, he was speaking of her cleavage.

My mom asked him, "Is it wrong to show that line?"

"It's not modest," he replied.

"What does it mean to be modest?" she asked, eagerly anticipating the answer.

He said, "You are not to squeeze them together like that. You are suppose to spread them apart as far as possible."

My parents spent the rest of the day recovering from stomach pains caused by laughter.

Ten to Thirteen Years Old

Teach them about their desires by saying the same thing about their desires that you said about their bodies: "God created your desires. They are not dirty. We all have them. You are normal."

Perhaps the single Shullamite woman from Song of Songs was around this age when she experienced intense sexual desire for Solomon. Her desire and passion spills over in one of the most graphic texts of your Bible:

> Let him kiss me with the kisses of his mouth—
> > for your love is more delightful than wine.
> Pleasing is the fragrance of your perfumes;
> > your name is like perfume poured out.
> > No wonder the maidens love you!
> Take me away with you—let us hurry!
> > Let the king bring me into his chambers. (Song 1:2–4)

Don't freak out when your son or daughter desires someone of the opposite sex. Talk it through, and be open about your own feelings at that age. Don't lock them in their bedroom or send them into hiding, because the more you freak out, the more you drive them to secrecy. It is critically important to keep the lines of communication open at this stage. Don't avoid the topics of masturbation, wet dreams, erections, pubic hair, fondling, kissing, petting, oral sex, and intercourse.

Fourteen Years Old and Up

Get them ready for marriage. This one is foreign to most parents I encounter in church today because to them it seems too early. Go with me for a second here.

You prepare them for college and for what it takes to get a job and make money. Let me ask you a question that will require a little bit of vision on your part. Picture your kids getting married and having children. Do you want to see your grandchildren during the holidays? Then prepare them for a great marriage.

Teach them to honor marriage, not just purity.

Parent Gut Check
- What is the scariest part of your children leaving home?
- In what ways are you not allowing your children to leave home?
- What "strings" do you need to start cutting?
- How will you respond to your child's desire to get a job?
- Can you think of a few differences between sports and jobs? When it comes to teaching responsibility, what do they have in common?

- Are you painting a beautiful picture of marriage for your children? If so, how?

Chapter 9

Great Parents, Lousy Lovers

Amy and I tend toward a kid-centered home, but we consciously fight against it every day. We know it's not good for us or for the kids. Parents of generations past used to remind their children regularly, "The world does not revolve around you."

The average woman speaks twenty thousand words a day, while the average man speaks seven thousand words a day. Amy and I both fit those gender stereotypes. I believe our daughter, however, can speak upward of fifty thousand words a day. She has a lot to say and loves good conversation. The challenge is teaching her when to use those words—that it is not the time to start a conversation when we order food at a drive-in, when Mommy and Daddy are talking to each other, or during a church service.

One Sunday when Corynn was four, she escaped from her class at church. I was in the middle of a passionate teaching point when I saw her waving at me from the back of the auditorium. I waved back and gave her a wink. That did not suffice, so she took it as permission to ask me a question right in the middle of the service.

As she walked down the center aisle, I got nervous. She walked right up onto the stage and asked me, "Have you seen Mom?"

Not only were we going to have a conversation, but the congregation would hear every word. Corynn spoke to me as though no one was there.

"Corynn, we are in the middle of the message, and I need you to go back to your class," I said.

"Daddy, Mom said Emma could come over after church, and I want to see if Lucy can too," she said.

With every eye in the room watching me, I got down on one knee and worked through our after-church social arrangements, then kissed Corynn good-bye.

Our worship pastor said it was the best part of that particular service. I was reminded of Abraham Lincoln and how he reportedly allowed his son Tad to interrupt his cabinet meetings. Tad was seven when his dad became president, and Lincoln occasionally interrupted meetings to interact with him.

The occasional interruption like this isn't a problem to me at all. Parents show concern and care for their children when they drop everything to meet an immediate need. It shows our children that they are a priority. Interrupting a football game on TV, stopping the mower for a chat, and even pausing in the middle of a sermon can show our children that they matter to us.

However, our children are not the number-one priority, and they need to know that. Corynn Mae Cunningham knows that she is my princess, but she also knows that Amy Kay Cunningham is the

Queen in our house. No one speaks when the Queen is talking. No one runs ahead of the Queen. When the Queen picks a restaurant or activity, no amount of whining from the kids deters me. Our course is set.

My wife likes being the Queen. The kids and I like her to be the Queen. But she rarely takes advantage of her esteemed position because she knows it destroys the lesson we are trying to teach Corynn. Regularly I hear Amy say, "Corynn, you need to find a man who treats you as well as your daddy treats me."

But Corynn is convinced that our home has enough room for two Queens. The fact is, there is room for only one.

I have the opportunity to spend a good bit of time on college campuses. I enjoy sharing with students in chapel, eating lunch with campus pastors, and walking the halls with professors and administrators. One conversation that repeats itself is that freshman students often experience great frustration in the first few weeks and months.

Johnnie Moore is a good friend and the campus pastor at Liberty University. He has a huge heart for the student body and desires to teach and encourage them toward a radical commitment to Christ. He shares with me how the brokenness of today's homes crushes his students. The absence of good models and their parents' struggling marriages or divorces leaves the students disjointed when they get on campus. Many of these freshman students grew up in kid-centered homes where Mom and Dad made one, two, or all three of the following mistakes.

First, the parents relaxed the rules and boundaries in an attempt to make up for rough times at home. Second, the parents placed undue relational burdens on the kids to make up for a struggling or failed marriage. Third, the parents gave too much privilege as a result of success or borrowed money.

In my many conversations with Johnnie, I see that one of the struggles on college campuses today is that professors, deans, pastors, and resident assistants become more like parents to the students. We call that mentoring, but the reality is that we ask college leaders to do what Mom and Dad abstained from: *teaching responsibility*.

There are several ways to identify whether your home is kid centered. It starts by understanding the priority of relationships and journeys.

There are four spiritual journeys in the home. Your own personal spiritual journey as a parent is your first priority. You must be connected to the Source of life in order to give to the other spiritual journeys in the home. The second spiritual journey is that of your spouse. Your goal is to serve your spouse without plugging into him or her as the source of life and without taking responsibility for his or her journey. Your spouse is 100 percent responsible for his or her own spiritual journey. Together you tend to the third spiritual journey in your home, your marriage journey, by enjoying a lifetime together. Then your own spiritual journey and your marriage journey paint a picture of the gospel of Jesus for your children and their spiritual journey.

Prioritize these journeys. If you start by tending to your child's journey first, you will create a kid-centered home that erodes every other journey in the house.

Your children have a front-row seat to your marriage. The two greatest gifts we can give our children are a mom and dad who enjoy life together, and the hope of a great marriage of their own. Paint a beautiful picture of marriage, which can be done both as a married or a single parent.

At Starbucks the other day my good friend announced to me that his daughter was done with her new marriage. His heart was heavy, and he wore the pain on his sleeve. And unfortunately, he's not the first guy to break that news to me; in fact I hear it all the time. However, this time it was different. His announcement came with a confession.

"My daughter came over to the house the other night and broke the news to her mom and me that she is leaving her husband of three years," he said.

"Did you see this coming?" I asked.

"We knew they were having problems but had no idea they would throw the towel in this quickly," he said. "She told me, 'Dad, I will not stay with him for the next thirty-plus years if it means we are going to have a marriage like you have with Mom. I just can't do it.' Ted, do you have any idea how hard that hit me?"

The primary reason young people give me today for quitting marriage early or for unnecessarily delaying marriage is their fear of ending up in a marriage like their parents'. Mom and Dad may stay committed and divorce-proof, but they do not display the qualities of honor, love, and enjoyment that will inspire their children to marry and stay married.

I see my fair share of struggling marriages. Every week at Woodland Hills Family Church, we work with couples who feel they have reached their end. They give up. One striking similarity I see in most couples today is that they have or desire a closer relationship with their children than they have with each other. When parents misunderstand the parent-child bond, their marriage and children suffer.

So give your children the gift of a great marriage.

Single Parents

Single parents tend to spoil their children. According to the Urban Dictionary, a Disney Dad is a "father (usually divorced or separated) who tries to compensate for his absence by giving his kids everything and taking them everywhere during visitation; a weekend father that lets his children do anything they want when they visit. Also gives them anything they want, creating very spoiled kids under the premise of not wanting them to be mad at him. Often the children boss the dad around, even yelling at him with no reprisals."[1]

Making up for a bad relationship or marriage by overindulging the children only equips them for a life of selfishness, pride, and ego. Instead, give them a model to follow that confesses mistakes and makes decisions that are rooted in Scripture.

Several years ago I preached a series of sermons out of 1 and 2 Timothy. In these letters the apostle Paul, an older pastor, writes to Timothy, a younger pastor, about the ups and downs of leading a church. I particularly love 1 Timothy 5 when he encourages Timothy to promote marriage among the single mothers in the church. It behooves church leaders today to challenge young men to consider marrying single moms.

I went after the young men in our church when we got to this chapter in Timothy. We even went so far as to offer to pay for the first dates of any young man who asked out a single mom. After all, there's no better way for the church to care for widows and orphans than to encourage men to marry the widows and then adopt their children. There is only one word for that kind of guy: *man*.

We were in 1 Timothy 5 for only a couple of weeks, but the emails started to flow into the office. This one caught my eye, and we decided to share it with the congregation:

> Ted ... good job in speaking out that our boys don't have much fight.... It's not normal to feminize both the girls and the boys, but our current culture seems to be doing that. Thanks for putting a little "fight" in the guys.
>
> And now about me ... how about encouraging the dating of "old" women in the church. Some of us are over forty ... really. Even over fifty and looking to go out to dinner or take a nice boat ride. I come with my own paycheck, home (lakefront), a couple of Sea-Doos, a teenager (she's pretty sweet most days). Where are the nice "old" guys for us ... they don't have to adopt my kid, just pay for dinner!
>
> Keep up the great work.[2]

When I finished reading the email to the congregation I asked, "Well, Woodland Hills, where are the old men?" Five guys stood up. One guy in the back took notice of his competition and immediately started dancing. The place erupted with laughter and cheers.

After the service several guys lined up and asked me to point out the woman from the email. One guy waited around for all the other guys to leave, then approached me and asked, "Do you have a picture of those Sea-Doos?" I jokingly told him, "Leave my presence because little boys make bad husbands."

I love being a part of a church that celebrates and promotes marriage. That is why I am continually encouraging single parents to free their hearts of anger. Unresolved anger is like drinking poison and expecting your ex to get sick. Allow the Holy Spirit to call you by name on this and point out any root of bitterness in your heart.

Jaded single parents also pose a serious threat to the future marriages of their children. Notice I did not say single parents. Jaded single parents make two mistakes. First, they assume that their child's marriage will go down the same path as their own failed marriage or relationship. Second, selfishness sets in, and they struggle to relinquish time with their child. A mom or dad with unresolved anger, bitterness, or resentment toward his or her former spouse can write negative and often false beliefs about marriage onto a child's heart.

Do not overlook love or a potential spouse because you want to throw all of your energy, time, and money into your child. I counsel single moms raising a single child to get married. It is not required, but it's definitely a blessing for your child to see a healthy marriage lived out daily before his or her very eyes.

Blended Families

Blended families are all about setting the right expectations on the front end. Starting with realistic expectations prevents misunderstandings and heartache. There are four types of blended families. Which one best reflects your family?

The blended-traditional family closely resembles the traditional family and is the best model to seek. Both parents understand that there needs to be open and honest communication between each other and the biological parents involved. Conversation over parenting styles should be frank and include the understanding that bonding as a family will take time. Tension and "side taking" is limited because the couple presents a united front to the children.

The blended-idealistic family lives with the fantasy that they will quickly create a perfect traditional family. In this case, usually two unique and different expectations must resolve. First, the blended family will never actually become a traditional family. Second, any attempt to move toward a blended-traditional family will take time. The false expectations of instant unity, peace, and perfect coparenting will lead to instant frustration.

The blended-matriarchal family presents a home where Mom runs the show and Dad follows her lead. Mom often expects Dad to become a best friend to the children. He is to know their whereabouts and the dos and don'ts of the child, but he is usually given clear limitations on discipline.

The blended-patriarchal family presents a home where Dad is large and in charge. Mom follows his lead in most areas but usually handles the discipline of her biological children. Much like the blended-matriarchal home, Mom still expects her husband to be a buddy to the children.

Work toward realistic expectations. The blended family will never be a traditional family, and cohesion between two families always takes time. And yes, even in the blended family, you must prioritize the marriage.

I encounter these differing scenarios through the weddings I perform for soon-to-be-blended families. I recall a recent wedding in particular. Mark was a single dad with a son and a daughter, and Angela was a single mom with two daughters. They met and fell in love through a mutual friend.

They dated for six months, and the engagement lasted only three. I had the opportunity to perform their wedding ceremony, which meant I also was their premarital counselor. My friend Kevin Leman once said, "Families don't blend; they collide." So with that quote in mind, I devoted an entire premarital session to the blending of these two unique families.

At the beginning of the session Angela told me, "We will get along just fine so long as Mark does not get in the way of me and the girls."

"If that is the case, then I can't marry you two," I responded.

"What do you mean?" she asked.

I said, "In order for you to have a successful marriage, Mark needs to come before your girls, and you need to come before his daughter and son. That is the only way it works. When you enter into a one-flesh love with Mark, the kids come second."

A good number of my weddings are that of blended families, and boy oh boy have I received some odd requests. One couple requested that I exchange vows between the parents and children. Another couple requested that I ask permission of the children for giving their mom away. Both requests lay an emotional burden on the children and place them in an unnecessary role.

I am all about giving the kids gifts and recognition at a wedding of this kind. However, in the ceremony I make it very clear that the universe will not revolve around the children.

Parents Who Adopt or Struggle with Infertility

My friends Steve and Jen struggled for years with infertility. The pain was palpable when you were in a room with them and someone mentioned the word *baby*. Mother's Day at church was a service they avoided.

Steve and Jen celebrated two major milestones at Woodland Hills. They became Christians at our church and got married shortly thereafter. However, the milestone of starting a family eluded them for years after their marriage.

They moved to Phoenix, Arizona, shortly after they married in Branson. I'll never forget getting the text message with the big news: "Baby on the way. Please pray that all goes well and the baby carries to term."

Several months later Sammy came into the world healthy, and we all celebrated.

Steve and Jen's prayers were answered.

Gary Smalley and I were in Phoenix for a marriage seminar right before Sammy turned one. I met him and dedicated him to the Lord all on the same day. We walked out to the courtyard of Mission Community Church on a warm and sunny afternoon and prayed the blood of Jesus over him, protection from evil, and that God would fulfill His purpose in Sammy's life.

Jen braced herself for what I had already been sharing with her in past conversations. My fear was Jen would embrace Sammy and prioritize him in the home above Steve. This is very common of parents who believe their child to be a miracle.

"Jen, what is the greatest gift you can give Sammy?" I asked.

"I know, I know, I know," she said. She was thinking but didn't say, *Ted, give me this moment without going all "marriage guy" on me.*

It is easy to unintentionally create a kid-centered home if you believe your child to be a miracle. Daily you remind yourself of the prayer and patience required to conceive this child. While we believe that all children are a blessing from the Lord, we begin to raise the value even higher for those who are "miracles." Parents who struggle with infertility and ultimately conceive have much in common with parents who adopt.

Many words come to mind when I think of adoption. Rescue. Adventure. Family. Mission. The excitement, emotion, and anticipation that surround the adoption process bond a couple. It happens often at Woodland Hills. Every so often we find ourselves at an airport, awaiting the arrival of a new member of our church family. We've greeted children from Russia, China, Ethiopia, and Rwanda.

There are many similarities between the adoptive couples and the couples who struggle with infertility but then by some miracle get pregnant. Some of my favorite stories actually combine the two. A couple tries for years to get pregnant, gives up, adopts a child, and *then* gets pregnant. Yeah, God!

Parents of Special Needs Children

Prioritizing your marriage is every bit as important for the couple raising a special-needs child. While your child may never leave your home, Genesis 2:24 still applies to you. The two of you must be one and secure the marriage bond.

I recently encouraged some couples with special-needs children while on Focus on the Family radio. I said, "Mom and Dad, I get it. You provide the absolute best possible care for your child. No one doubts that. However, you need to lean in on and request some second-best care from your parents, friends, and church family. They are there, ready to give you a much-needed break. Leave your children in capable hands, and enjoy a night on the town together. Refuel and recharge so you have something to give tomorrow."

Honor and Enjoy

There are two passages of Scripture that every couple needs to memorize: Hebrews 13:4 and Ecclesiastes 9:7–9.

To become a great parent and great lover, start by esteeming marriage as highly valuable. Hebrews 13:4 says, "Marriage should be honored by all, and the marriage bed kept pure, for God will judge the adulterer and all the sexually immoral."

There is a concept called confirmation bias. Basically, it's the idea that we make decisions, then look for the evidence to back up those decisions. So you must avoid all thoughts pertaining to your spouse such as *Ball and chain*, or *We stay married for the kids*, and *We stay married because she puts up with me*. Change your tone. Speak only words of high honor about your spouse and marriage. Give your children something to look forward to, not something to fear.

Make the decision that marriage is great, important, and valuable, and then spend your lifetime seeking out and discovering the evidence to back up your decision. When you honor marriage, you will find ways to enjoy marriage.

Ecclesiastes is an often-avoided book of the Bible because people find it depressing. Chapter 1 starts with Solomon painting a picture of the earth being a grinder that you and I are born into: "Generations come and generations go, but the earth remains forever" (1:4). Life is a grind. No matter how much money you make, there is no buying your way out of the grinder. No matter how much education you receive, there is no outsmarting the grinder.

The grinder will eventually cause your body to break down. The secret is to keep your attitude from the grinder while your body is in the midst of it. Young people are challenged in this book to commit their lives to God before they get old and death approaches:

> Remember your Creator
> > in the days of your youth,
> before the days of trouble come
> > and the years approach when you will say,
> > "I find no pleasure in them." (12:1)

You're in the grind all the way to the end, and your only way out of the grinder is death. Encouraged yet? In the midst of the grind, God wants you to enjoy your life:

> Go, eat your food with gladness, and drink your
> wine with a joyful heart, for it is now that God
> favors what you do. Always be clothed in white,
> and always anoint your head with oil. (9:7–8)

God wants us to enjoy life in the midst of the grind. We must laugh in the midst of the grind (3:4). Dare I say that part of your purpose in life is to play and have fun? Enjoying life is part of life! God did not give you your spouse as part of the grind. He gave you this person so you could enjoy life with your spouse in the midst of the grind:

> Enjoy life with your wife, whom you love, all the
> days of this meaningless life that God has given you
> under the sun—all your meaningless days. For this
> is your lot in life and in your toilsome labor under
> the sun. (9:9)

This is the only place in the Bible where it says, "Enjoy life with your wife." No need to choose between the two. One does not trump the other. You can have both because marriage enhances life. Walk together, travel together, eat gourmet meals together, and go to a wine tasting. Find ways every day to enjoy life together.

Spice It Up

In 2009, Woodland Hills Family Church partnered with Mission Community Church in Phoenix, Arizona, to launch a brand-new marriage ministry called TwoIgnite. The strategy of TwoIgnite is simple. We take one Sunday a month and teach couples and singles how to honor, enjoy, and prioritize their marriages. Rather than giving couples a DVD and a workbook and plugging them into a small group, we send them out to enjoy life with each other. Not only have couples from our church reported back higher levels of marital satisfaction since implementing this practice, but Amy and I personally have grown like crazy in our own marriage.

The following twenty activities are taken directly from our TwoIgnite ministry. They offer some fun and creative ways to spice up your marriage. If you're neglecting your marriage because of the kids, pick a couple activities from the list and start immediately prioritizing your marriage.

1. Create a Lovemaking Playlist

You remember love tapes, otherwise known as mix tapes? You recorded your favorite music and gave it to the one you dated.

Download your favorite love songs and create an actual playlist called "Lovemaking Playlist." It needs to have at least four or five songs. Two songs for foreplay and two to three songs for making love. And don't stop with one playlist. Date the playlists or even create different playlists for special occasions.

2. Double the Frequency

This is as simple as it sounds. If you make love once a week, commit to doing it twice this week. If you are a two to three times a week couple, then it looks like you will only have one day of rest.

Keep in mind—sex is a barometer of the marriage. More sex does not guarantee a better marriage. However, increasing the frequency requires you to rearrange your schedule and habits to make time for lovemaking. Couples who increase frequency tend to report higher levels of marital satisfaction.

3. Walk Down Memory Lane

Bust open those yearbooks and wedding albums. Discuss old friends, classes, favorite teachers, sports, and clothing. Don't forget to admire those hairstyles.

What do you miss about those days?

What do you miss least?

If you could go back, what would you change?

4. Host a Wine and Cheese Tasting for Two

Make this simple or fancy, cheap or expensive, red or white.

You need only to open one bottle and pair it with a couple pieces of cheese for the night. Enjoy it as a late-night snack or even as a replacement for your regular dinner. Either way, put a little planning into the evening. Ask your spouse about his or her preferred wine and cheese, then bring that and also try something new.

5. Cook a Gourmet Meal

Gourmet is about small portions and presentation. Most of our meals at home are fast, large portions. Plan a four-course meal and prepare it together. Spend a day or two at the beginning of the week planning this meal, take another day to shop together for it, and at the end of the week prepare the meal together.

Think fresh. Get fresh fish, or buy your bread from a bakery. Get the makings for a salad from an open-air market.

Cook, plate, and even drizzle the sauce. Put some love into the meal. Enjoy.

6. Lighten Up

A cheerful heart is good medicine. Laughter makes all things tolerable. "Laugh out loud," said Chuck Swindoll. "It helps flush out the nervous system." On another occasion Chuck said, "Laughter is the most beautiful and beneficial therapy God ever granted humanity."

Bob Hope said that laughter is an "instant vacation." Bill Cosby said, "If you can find humor in anything, you can survive it."

Here are several ways you can bring some laughter into your marriage:

> Download a joke, memorize it, and retell it to your spouse.
> Watch a clean comedian on TV.
> Watch a funny movie together.
> Find a creative way to poke fun at yourself.
> Fake it! Just start laughing for no reason at all. It's
>   contagious!

7. Sell on eBay for Missions

Start by picking a missionary, neighbor, nonprofit organization, or church project that you and your spouse are passionate about. Set a goal for a gift you would like to make to that charity.

Gather up unused or unwanted items from around your house and garage and sell them through an online auction.

8. Go on a Double Date

Invite another couple to join you on your weekly date. Couple chemistry is sometimes hard, so invite a couple with whom you both have good chemistry.

9. Rearrange the Furniture

Variety is the spice of life, and too often we get stuck in ruts. The home often becomes a perfect metaphor for the marriage.

Pick a room in your house and completely rearrange it. Change out pictures, move furniture, add lighting, and stage the room. If you don't like it, change it back at the end of the week.

10. Make an Honor List

You can build honor and security in your marriage through confirmation bias. Here's the secret: when you make a decision about someone, your feelings follow. People tend to only see what they believe.

Get a legal pad out and begin listing every positive quality you can think of about your spouse. You should be able to come up with a few pages. Here are some questions to get you started:

> What about your spouse originally turned you on?
> What makes your spouse laugh?
> What makes your spouse cry?
> When does he/she display the most compassion?
> When does he/she act the most like Jesus?
> How does he/she honor people?

11. Do a Marriage Checkup

Every woman has a built-in marriage manual. That's the phrase I use to describe the innate desire every woman has for a great relationship. One of the ways you can find out how your marriage is going is to ask each other the following three big questions. Each person should feel comfortable sharing the answers to these questions honestly, knowing the responses are designed to help improve and strengthen your relationship.

1. On a scale of 1 to 10, what kind of marriage do you want?
2. On a scale of 1 to 10, where is our marriage today?
3. What would it take today or in the next few weeks to move our relationship to a 10?

12. Write a Scripture-Based Note to Your Spouse

When was the last time you wrote a love note to your spouse, just letting him or her know your thoughts and feelings? In order to spice it up a little, take the verse from Song of Songs 4:1–15 and rewrite the passage in your own words for your spouse. You may even want to select some special paper or pens to craft your love note.

13. Make Time for Quarterly Marriage Realignment (QMR)

In the busyness of life, it's easy to allow issues to remain unresolved. Whether the issues are about parenting, bills, planning, sexual interest, or household duties, some issues can go untouched for too long. That's why it's important to have a regular meeting time and place where it's safe for you and your spouse to discuss issues.

Sometime this week, plan a QMR with your spouse. Give each other a few days' notice so you can prayerfully think about issues and details that may have been swept under the rug in the rush of life. Open this time together with prayer. Commit to really listen to each other, speak words thoughtfully and in love, and know that the goal of this time is to strengthen your marriage.

14. Demonstrate a Servant's Heart

Over the course of the next week, look for ten small things you can do to serve your spouse without any expectation of acknowledgement or even appreciation. Go above and beyond to pay attention to your spouse's desires, needs, and even simple whims. At the end of the week, write down how these small acts of kindness affected your heart as well as your spouse's heart.

15. Read Song of Solomon Aloud with Your Spouse This Week

Dive into this passionate book of the Bible with your spouse and explore its meaning. While reading, look at the portrait God draws of a man and woman in love. Talk about what you learn with your spouse.

16. Prayer Challenge

Pray together as a couple every day for the next seven days.

Our informal polls at marriage events reveal that less than 20 percent of professing Christian couples pray together on a regular basis. Outside of meal times, find time every day to pray.

Pray for your children, your church, our nation's leaders, missionaries, and your friends. Thank the Lord for who He is and what He has done in your life. Cry out to the Lord with your struggles.

Don't be afraid to write down your prayers ahead of time. In other words, make your prayer time intentional and devotional.

17. Budget Challenge

Pick a mission, organization, or church project that you support. Cut fifty to one hundred dollars out of your budget this week and give it to the mission, organization, or church next week. Think through every purchase this week. It doesn't require many cuts in discretionary spending, coffee runs, or dinners out to make a significant impact in the life of another person.

18. Blessing Challenge

Prepare a written blessing for your spouse and read it in front of your children. (If your children live in a distant state, email it to them under the heading "Why I married your mom/dad.")

19. Kissing Week

Did you know that you burn two to three calories with a romantic kiss? While that should not be our primary reason for kissing, most couples need to kiss more. Kissing improves your health and marriage.

Kissing has many forms. There's the "I'm sick and don't want to give you germs" air kiss. There is the "I'm feeling a cold coming on and want to be careful" peck on the cheek. It is a cousin to the "I know you are mad at me" peck on the cheek. You have your "good-bye" and "good night" kiss that always feel the same and a bit rushed. There's the long, passionate, and deep kissing that says, "I hope tonight is the night."

Spend time each day giving one another extended kisses.

20. NST (Nonsexual Touching) Week

NSTs includes a hand on the shoulder as you say, "Thank you for dinner." It is a hand on the small of the back for a picture or an assist to a seat. How a spouse responds to NSTs communicates much to you and the kids. A relaxed, non-angry person likes to be touched. An angry person avoids touching or advances toward anything physical. NSTs can also include just standing close together.

Hugging can be either nonsexual or sexual. There is the embrace that lasts longer than the hug you give Aunt Myrtle. The embrace tells your spouse that things are good and we can relax together. It also communicates that "I am not in a rush, and I have nowhere to be." Your spouse knows immediately how distracted you are by the length and intensity of the hug.

I also believe that hand holding is a lost art. Most of our hand holding occurs in the car or in the movie theater. There is the interlocking finger approach that requires immediate participation in order to work. The wrap-around-the-palm approach is most often used to test the waters after a fight. You make an initial squeeze and wait for one back. No squeeze means no forgiveness yet. Then you have the hand holding thermostat to deal with. We do not hold hands for longer than five minutes due to sweaty palm syndrome. You can tell you know your lover when you both agree it is over at the same time.

Commit this week to give your spouse twelve NSTs each day. Spread them out throughout the day.

Parent Gut Check

- Who comes first in your home—your spouse or your kids? Do your kids rule the roost? What steps will you take in eradicating the kid-centered home? What steps are necessary to presenting a united front with your spouse?
- Do you enjoy life with your spouse? In what ways?
- When you prioritize your marriage in the home, what does it communicate to your children?

Scripture Index

Isaiah 40:31

Proverbs 16:24

Matthew 19:24

Proverbs 26:11

Isaiah 40:31

Song of Songs 2:15

Matthew 23:24

Revelation 19:11

Psalm 50:11

Proverbs 11:22

Genesis 2:17

John 1:29

Song of Songs 1:9

Genesis 2:25

Proverbs 28:13

1 John 1:9

James 5:16

Psalm 102:6–7

Luke 15:16

Psalm 105:39–41

Genesis 9:14–15

Numbers 30:2

Genesis 3:4–5

James 1:13–15

Psalm 1:1–3

Revelation 22:18

Proverbs 30:17

Exodus 20:12

Ephesians 6:2–3

Luke 10:3

Proverbs 14:4

2 Corinthians 6:14

Deuteronomy 22:10

Genesis 6:19

Hebrews 11:7

Chapter 6

John 3:16

Romans 10:9–10

John 14:21, 23–24

John 14:6

John 14:7

John 5:39–40

Psalm 78:1–4

Matthew 28:19–20

Mark 8:36

John 13:14–15

Matthew 10:32–33

Hebrews 13:7

Chapter 7

Ephesians 2:2

Colossians 1:13

2 Timothy 2:26

Genesis 3:4–5

Mark 7:18–23

Notes

Chapter 1: Trophies

1. "Perfect Parents—Trophy Kids," *UAB Publications*, http://main.uab.edu/show.asp?durki=91311, accessed March 29, 2012.
2. Carl E. Pickhardt, PhD, "Vanity Parenting and Adolescent Performance," *Psychology Today*, February 21, 2011, www.psychologytoday.com/blog/surviving-your-childs-adolescence/201102/vanity-parenting-and-adolescent-performance.

Chapter 2: Trophy Parents

1. Used with permission.
2. Pickhardt, "Vanity Parenting and Adolescent Performance," *Psychology Today*.
3. Oxford Dictionaries, s.v. "narcissism," http://oxforddictionaries.com/definition/narcissism?region=us.
4. "Perfect Parents—Trophy Kids," *UAB Publications*.
5. Diana Baumrind, "The Influence of Parenting Style on Adolescent Competence and Substance Use," *Journal of Early Adolescence* (1991), 11, no. 1.
6. Baumrind, "The Influence of Parenting Style on Adolescent Competence and Substance Use," *Journal of Early Adolescence*.

7. Investopedia, s.v. "ROI," www.investopedia.com/terms/r/returnoninvestment.asp.

Chapter 3: Know Limits

1. "Overscheduled Kids," *Putting Family First*, www.puttingfamilyfirst.org/overscheduled_kids.php, accessed June 20, 2012.
2. "Statistics," www.facebook.com/statistics, accessed November 2011 (page discontinued).
3. "#numbers," Twitter Blog, March 14, 2011, http://blog.twitter.com/2011/03/numbers.html.
4. Sarah Evans, "50 Social Media Stats to Kickstart Your Slide Deck," *Advertising Age*, July 15, 2011, http://adage.com/article/adagestat/50-social-media-stats-kickstart-slide-deck/228708/.
5. New York Times' Customer Insight Group, "The Psychology of Sharing," September 19, 2011, 16–20, http://www.scribd.com/doc/65545180/The-New-York-Times-The-Psychology-of-Sharing-study-in-partnership-with-Latitude-Research.
6. New York Times' Customer Insight Group, "The Psychology of Sharing," 13, 15.
7. Sanity Rose, "Social Networking Addiction," Yahoo! Voices, August 2, 2009, http://voices.yahoo.com/social-networking-addiction-3934638.html.

Chapter 4: Everything Jesus Said about Children and Parents

1. *Braveheart*, directed by Mel Gibson (Paramount, 2000), DVD.

Chapter 5: Spiritual Journeys

1. Matt Gumm. Used with permission.
2. Paul Lee Tan, *Encyclopedia of 7700 Illustrations*, #4174 (Rockville, MD: Assurance Publishers, 1998), 960.

3. Howard Hendricks, source information unknown.

4. Kristofor Husted, "Can Frequent Family Dinners Help Teens Resist Drugs?" Shots: NPR's Health Blog, September 22, 2011, www.npr.org/blogs/health/2011/09/22/140705512/can-frequent -family-dinners-help-teens-resist-drugs?ps=sh_stcathdl.

Chapter 6: Kids Who Follow Jesus

1. Dean Seaborn, "Legacy of Faith: Part 2," *Focus on the Family Daily*, September 7, 2011, www.focusonthefamily.com/radio. aspx?ID={57B8F3DE-090A-4E32-AC13-0BA2B7F41189}.

2. Haley Tooms, Facebook post. Used with permission.

Chapter 7: Preparing Our Children for the World

1. Used with permission.

2. The National Commission on Terrorist Attacks upon the United States, *The 9/11 Commission Report* (New York: W. W. Norton & Co., 2004), xvi.

Chapter 8: Adult Milestones

1. *The World Book Dictionary* (Chicago: World Book, Inc., 2003), 120.

2. Ron Alsop, *The Trophy Kids Grow Up* (San Francisco, CA: Jossey-Bass, 2008), 6–7, 15.

3. "Perfect Parents—Trophy Kids," *UAB Publications*.

Chapter 9: Great Parents, Lousy Lovers

1. "Disney Dad," Urban Dictionary, July 2009, www.urbandictionary. com/define.php?term=disney%20dad.

2. Used with permission.